Judge Fuchs and the Boston Braves, 1923–1935

Judge Fuchs
and the
Boston Braves,
1923–1935

ROBERT S. FUCHS *and* WAYNE SOINI

To Fred Peterson –
A "Cover" who ought
to have managed
the Braves –
if he did, they'd
still be in
Boston!
– Wayne Soini

McFarland & Company, Inc., Publishers
Jefferson, North Carolina and London

Front cover photo: Judge Fuchs on the dugout steps during his tenure as manager of the Braves (from the Robert S. Fuchs Collection).

Library of Congress Cataloguing-in-Publication Data

Fuchs, Robert S., 1912–
    Judge Fuchs and the Boston Braves, 1923–1935 / by Robert S. Fuchs and Wayne Soini.
        p.   cm.
    Includes index.

    ISBN-13: 978-0-7864-0482-7
    (softcover : 50# alkaline paper) ∞

    1. Fuchs, Judge, d. 1961.   2. Baseball team owners —
Massachusetts — Biography.   3. Boston Braves (Baseball team)
— History.   I. Soini, Wayne, 1948–   . II. Title.
GV865.F793A3   1998
796.357'092 — dc21
[B]   97-50028

British Library cataloguing data are available

Manufactured in the United States of America

McFarland & Company, Inc., Publishers
  Box 611, Jefferson, North Carolina 28640
   www.mcfarlandpub.com

Dedicated to the Boston Chapter of the Baseball Writers' Association of America, which for over sixty years has kept alive the memory of Judge Fuchs both by hosting the annual Baseball Writers' Dinner, initiated by the Judge, and by the Judge Emil E. Fuchs Memorial Award, recipients of which include Ernie Banks, Bill McKechnie, Walter Alston, Bob Gibson, Carl Yastrzemski, Joe Cronin, Warren Spahn, Hank Aaron, Whitey Ford, Robin Roberts, Eddie Mathews, Rod Carew, Willie Mays, Earl Weaver, Frank Robinson, Brooks Robinson, Louis Aparicio and Tom Seaver. Sixteen of the recipients have been inducted into the Hall of Fame in Cooperstown.

The authors wish to express their deep appreciation to the author of the excellent *Braves Encyclopedia* (Philadelphia: Temple University Press, 1995) for his gracious cooperation in highlighting the activities of the Braves circa 1923–1935.

Table of Contents

Preface
by Wayne Soini

I want to introduce you to the first person who applied the term "screwball" to pitching: Bob Fuchs.

Bob, business manager of the Braves' farm team in Harrisburg in 1932 and 1933, in 1934 became team president. What change did this make? Bob says it meant he got to drive the team's bus. But he also spoke for the team and one day Bob was interviewed by Paul Gallico. Gallico asked Bob about the team's pitchers. When Bob mentioned Hefflefinger as a "screwball" pitcher, Gallico asked for a definition. Bob replied that a "screwball" is a "righthander who thinks left-handed." It passed from Bob to Gallico to print and the word has remained in circulation to this day.

I am very grateful to have helped shape this book from the Judge's personal journals that Bob owns, several volumes of scrapbooks and photos and, most importantly, Bob's own recollections.

Bob always had a talent for communication. In fact, the Judge had hoped for Bob to go into journalism. He arranged that his college freshman son would spend his summer studying sports writing with a master, John Kieran of the *New York Times.* However, at the beginning of his apprenticeship Bob attended a game in Harrisburg.

"It was only an exhibition game," Bob recalled, "but for me it was where to be. It was a great thrill. Baseball just had it all over typing on pieces of paper. I could type in college. In the summer, it was baseball I wanted. My father agreed to let me switch majors or, more properly stated, switch minors, from a minor in reporting to the minor leagues."

By keeping scrapbooks on the Judge and the Boston Braves, Bob had begun following his father's baseball years when he was a child. Reaching college years, Bob literally worked with his father and had an insider's view of the final three years of the Judge's ownership of the Braves. His unique

1

background kept him in contact with Boston Braves players and their families even up to the present day as the virtual sole surviving representative of the team of that era. Only with his assistance could this book be authoritative and accurate. What follows is a portrait of a fan.

It had to be because Judge Fuchs was not so much an owner, a manager or a player of baseball (although he was all of these) as he was the quintessential baseball fan. In the right city at the right time — at the Creation — he shared a box with up-and-coming playwright George M. Cohan at the Polo Grounds in the first World Series. He congratulated Christy Mathewson and sought out Connie Mack to talk about the game afterwards. Within a few years he was lawyer for John McGraw's champions, the Giants. When the game got its first commissioner, Kenesaw Mountain Landis, the Judge confronted the "baseball czar" over Benny Kauff, expelled from baseball for life. The Judge owned the Braves in the twenties and lost them in the thirties. In the forties manpower shortages on the home front led him to serve as a baseball writer for Boston papers. Thereafter he watched games from the press box at Braves Field and Fenway Park. When he died in 1961 he had lived a storied life, a baseball fan's dream.

In a way, his biography is the Everyman story, except that it is "Everyfan," an Everyfan who knew and did business with virtually all of the greats of baseball's golden age. This book is only an attempt to tell the story of a storied life.

Wayne Soini
Brookline, Massachusetts

Introduction

by Robert S. Fuchs

Who was Emil Fuchs?

He was my father.

But, as "Judge" Fuchs, he led a very public life.

The Judge is remembered for Sunday baseball, for introducing "Ladies Days" to Boston, for starting the annual dinner for Boston sports writers and, most warmly, for creating the old "Knot Hole Gang," by which youngsters saw major league baseball at Braves Field for only a nickel.

There are funny stories from my father's happy early days of ownership during the roaring twenties. And there's a First Division streak culminated by an exciting pennant race against the Giants in 1933. But in 1935, midway through the Great Depression, the Judge ran out of funds and was compelled to give up the Braves.

Although the saddest, this was not the Judge's first separation from the game. The Judge had known baseball since playing it on Sundays at Maspeth Park in New York in the 1890s. At age 13 he became catcher on the University Settlement House team. He was one of the varsity nine fielded by the College of the City of New York. A New Yorker looking for a career, he turned semi-pro with a minor league team out of Morristown, New Jersey. Injured, he had reluctantly hung up his glove and started law school nights while working as a managing clerk at the attorney general's office days.

He came to know politics. As New York's youngest deputy attorney general, appointed as soon as he took and passed the bar exam, he took on Tammany Hall, fighting over election results. He came to know politicians like Al Smith, Jimmy Walker and Fiorello LaGuardia. He made a name for himself, literally, as a judge on the old Municipal Court. During World War I the Judge factored inflation into his fines, not increasing them but cutting

3

Judge Emil E. Fuchs (from the Robert S. Fuchs Collection).

them for defendants hard-pressed to buy bread. Also during his three-year tenure, he found over 500 jobs for defendants otherwise headed for jail.

Once off the bench, his law practice really took off; at one point 15 clerks staffed his Chambers Street offices. Word spread that the Judge was unbeatable, that he never lost a jury trial. Despite success in court, he settled cases and at least once appealed to avoid a trial altogether. That was when

Christy Mathewson, Jr., Judge Fuchs and his close friend, Will Rogers, in St. Petersburg, Florida, circa 1927 (from the Robert S. Fuchs Collection).

he appealed a notorious gambler's indictment for murder. Arguing that the operator of a gambling concern does not thereby incur criminal responsibility if police officers are killed during a raid on the concern, the Judge was persuasive. The high court vacated the grand jury's indictment because there was no evidence directly linking the gambler with the fatal shots. The gambler who never stood trial was Arnold Rothstein, best remembered today as the gambler behind the 1919 "Black Sox" scandal.

The Judge not only won criminal cases but civil suits as well, and did office work. It was the Judge who wrote up the contract by which Will Rogers, then a cowboy philosopher with the Ziegfeld Follies, came to be owner of his first horse. It was the Judge who drew up the purchase agreement by which John McGraw and two partners became owners of the New York Giants. Known as a New York lawyer, the Judge's life became a tale of two cities, of New York and of Boston, once he bought the Braves. For several years he practiced law in New York while commuting. Finally, he moved to Boston with his family, where he stayed the rest of his life.

The Judge kept the Braves in Boston, resisting all offers to sell the franchise. Besides baseball itself, the Judge had come to love Boston. And the Braves' own goofs on the field, of course, insulated the team from much spirited bidding. However, I vouch for the fact that my father would not have sold his then–First Division team to Henry Ford when that industrial titan personally scouted the Braves but — in a story told here — Fate literally dropped the ball. Ford would have moved the Braves to Detroit.

Between 1923 and 1935 the Judge went through a fortune shoring up the Braves in their misfortunate era. They never won a pennant and, most seasons, battled over rights to the cellar of the National League. But the Judge never worried, retained his composure except when he rooted with enthusiasm and made warm friendships never later lost. He lost money but not friends or his love of the game.

This book is about the Judge's term of stewardship when the Braves played out of Braves Field, before night games, before Sunday baseball, radio just starting, when the grass was real and the players were steel.

Christy Mathewson, Babe Ruth, Rabbit Maranville, Rogers Hornsby, Johnny Evers, Wally Berger, Burleigh Grimes, George Sisler, Bill McKechnie, Rube Marquard, Casey Stengel, John McGraw, Branch Rickey, Connie Mack, William Wrigley, Colonel Jacob Ruppert, Commissioner Kenesaw Mountain Landis and others less well-known, populated the Judge's world. The Judge dictated stories of some of them for an autobiography he never completed. Never published, his stories provided the basis for this book. Not a full-length portrait of the Judge or of the Braves of the twenties and thirties, it is, I believe, nonetheless a fuller account than anyone has ever offered of either.

I want to conclude with a story outside the boundaries of the topic of the book, of the Judge 25 years after he lost the Braves, when the two threads of my father's life, baseball and politics, came together. It was 1960. John Kennedy was running for president. He was the second Catholic candidate. The first, Al Smith, had lost and some blamed the religious issue for that loss. In any case, in 1960 the religious issue was a worry. The Judge, crippled by arthritis, thought of Bob Hunter. Bob had pitched on Sundays at Maspeth Field to catcher Emil Fuchs. And Bob's family of church leaders included Anson Phelps Stokes, whom my father had befriended in New York and whose son was in 1960 the Episcopal Bishop of New England. My father contacted Stokes. The Bishop's resulting condemnation of "bloc voting" was widely publicized and has been credited with reducing Protestant backlash to a supposed Catholic "bloc vote." John Kennedy sent his personal letter of thanks to the Judge, along with an invitation to the Inaugural. The Judge, too ill to attend, died in late 1961. He was pleased to think that, in an election so close, he had helped score a run from behind the plate.

With this much of an introduction, I give you my father, Judge Fuchs, and his Boston Braves, 1923–1935.

Robert S. Fuchs
Chestnut Hill, Massachusetts

1

New York, New York

"The Polo Grounds, Ebbets Field, Yankee Stadium. Baseball was a reason for a person to live in New York. You could put up with a lot. The benefit was that your prayers as a fan were answered most seasons."
— Bob Fuchs (1995)

"Ebbets Field produced the most sentimental fans in history. They came to root or to hoot, but they came. When 'de bums' moved to California there was, thereafter, no joy in Bumville."
— Judge Fuchs, quoted in *Miami News* (June 28, 1958)

Baseball is said to have been conceived in upstate New York, and to have become a business first in Cincinnati. But wherever it was conceived, and wherever paid admissions were first charged technically, baseball was born and reborn as a professional sport in New York City.

Before the Civil War editors sent reporters out to baseball games held between competing amateur teams. After the Civil War editors sent reporters out to baseball games held between competing professional teams. Between 1870 and 1900 the free publicity and "reserve clause" contracts developed team identities. Certainly, some fans bonded with losing teams but, for the most part, the masses followed the winners. There was such stress placed on winning that a trend toward dirty tricks and violence characterized the games of this period.

Fans caustically celebrated the "mugs," or gangsters. One John McGraw, son of a coal miner, at 12 a runaway, drew attention with his aggressive tactics. So hell-bent to win, he played regardless of which rules or bones he broke. The bleachers taunted "Muggsy" mercilessly. McGraw, tough, violent and colorful, responded in a loud and outspoken way. McGraw's questionable moves were not all accomplished on the field or during games. He

Judge Fuchs (standing, third from right) was a catcher on the University Settlement Baseball Club in New York. Many sons of immigrants belonged to this East Side group, including Eddie Cantor, Supreme Court Justice Felix Frankfurter and Al Jolson (from the Robert S. Fuchs Collection).

loved to tell how he had once outwitted the great pitcher Rube Waddell. Waddell, about to pitch his first game for Philadelphia, was McGraw's target. McGraw, then playing for Baltimore, approached Waddell with the boast that he (McGraw) had the best arm in baseball. Waddell asserted that he had never heard of McGraw and gladly accepted McGraw's challenge. Each would throw a hundred balls to the fence. The one who hit the fence most won. Waddell won easily but faded in the first inning of the following game, exhausted by McGraw's "off-the-wall" contest. McGraw exemplified the competitive world of baseball at the time. It was a jungle in which no player went unbloodied. Umpires were both necessary and hated. Umpire-baiting erupted after every close call, and every call was close. This was an era of "survival of the fittest," "win at any price," "Devil take the hind-most," and "a lot of others out there want your job."

Outside the majors, amateurs continued to cultivate baseball as sport. Indeed, baseball was the name of the game for immigrants to become good citizens. "Settlement houses" sponsored uniformed teams and provided equipment and instruction to teams whose players constituted a cross-section of the Lower East Side. Visible on one of the most visible teams was catcher Emil Fuchs, who arrived from Bromberg, Germany, as a child, son of an Orthodox Jewish couple, who caught pitches from Bob Hunter, son of a family with Catholic and Episcopalian branches. Fuchs, the brilliant son of a chemist, had no greater ambition than to play baseball for the rest of his life. But after an injury, he took up the then-new game of auction bridge — and, for an occupation, law books.

He quickly became both a master in bridge and an expert in New York election laws. People marveled at the speed of his play and his decision-making pace in court. He acted so precipitously as to seem an impulsive man. But appearances were deceiving: Fuchs analyzed sequentially and almost instantly the options he had, discarded all but the best. To call this "impulsive" would be inaccurate; he was made to be a judging machine. He served briefly as a real judge, but the name was his ever after. Finally, practicing law around the game of games, his first love, baseball, offered him a lucrative and highly compatible way to make a living. As lawyer for the New York Giants, Judge Fuchs spent the morning at work, the afternoon at the ball game, then went home to his family on Riverside Drive. The Judge was at home in New York as the twenties started to roar. It was impossible for him to walk up Broadway without running into clients, friends and acquaintances.

By late 1922 he had reason to be satisfied. He had come a long way from the walk-up apartment he shared with his German-speaking family in the 1880s. He was one of New York's best and best-known lawyers. Newspaper readers could follow his cases in headlines. When New York Governor Whitman's election in 1918 was challenged in court, the Judge had been the one who successfully defended the result. The Judge had represented the powerful and the powerless, saints and sinners, millionaires and misfits, toting up an enviable record. He was one of the world's most cosmopolitan men in the most cosmopolitan city on the face of the earth. And he was going to dinner at the invitation of John McGraw, formerly known as "Muggsy," his employer. For the Judge represented the world champions. He was the lawyer for the New York Giants.

2

John McGraw's Invitation

"You could never tell him anything so far as baseball was concerned."
— Judge Fuchs on John McGraw

The ruler of the baseball world owed his friend a team. The ruler, the King of Diamonds by any standard, dominated the game as no manager ever had or ever would again — not even himself, after 1922. But as 1922 ended John McGraw was in his prime at the top of his game managing the best team in the world, the New York Giants. Not only had his team captured the National League pennant (tying the consecutive-pennant record) and gone on to win the World Series (as in 1921), the Series had been a spectacular triumph over the Yankees.

Apart from squeezing out a tie through the ally of darkness in a game called when the ball could no longer be seen, the Yankees in daylight had lost every game. Although it was not the four-game sweep invented by the "Miracle Braves" of Boston in 1914, it paired nicely with the only other four-wins-and-a-tie Series in history, put together in 1907 by the Tinker-to-Evers-to-Chance Chicago Cubs.

Johnny Evers loved to spin tales, among them were a few Bob Fuchs can recall vividly. He told how he and Tinkers disliked each other. On the first ball hit to Tinkers at the outset of the season with a man on first, Tinkers shot the ball to second base before Evers could get there and made him look like a fool. The next time the double play situation came up Evers was there on time! The same course of action was taken by Evers. When he got the ball he threw it with full force to second and Tinkers had to get there on time. Thus, the greatest double play combination in baseball was evolved. Johnny mentioned that at the end of the season a mutual friend got them to shake hands in a bar — and they never achieved quite the same results thereafter.

There was also the famous Merkel Boner when, with a man on third and Merkel on first, the batter hit a clean single to center field and the winning run scored from third gave the Giants the pennant. But Merkel took off from first base to the centerfield club house, not bothering to travel to second and Johnny Evers grabbed the field umpire, dragged him to center field, picked up the ball and dragged him back to second base. He touched the base and the winning run did not score. (There had been two outs at the time.) That night Evers' life was threatened. It was widely publicized and Evers' mother begged him (by telephone) not to play the next day. Worried, Evers called a cousin of his who was a subsheriff in New York. The next day with two outs and Chicago leading, the batter hit the ball to Tinkers, who threw to Chance for the final out. As soon as the ball was hit, Evers turned to run to the centerfield club house. As he turned he says the catcher Kling passed him en route to the club house. Suddenly Evers was surrounded by some of the toughest men he had ever seen — and he thought he'd had it. However, the men surrounding him turned out to be his cousin's gang from the sheriff's office. Evers states that the fans pelted the club house and the Chicago team was unable to leave it until nine o'clock that night!

The Giants' 1922 championship was credited not to nine players or to three players but to one manager: John McGraw. The baseball was a tool in McGraw's hands; the pitcher pitched what McGraw called, most of which were curve balls (as stated to Bob Fuchs by Larry Benton). He claimed credit for reducing Babe Ruth to impotence during the Series. Ruth, who hit no home runs in 17 at-bats, wilted to a paltry .118 before McGraw. And McGraw's attention to detail did not stop at calling every pitch but encompassed the entire playing field and beyond.

In this beyond-the-field realm McGraw and the Judge had taken opposing sides in 1921. Although he always called himself a "bad businessman," the Judge had recommended extending the Yankees' lease on the Polo Grounds. The 1920 Yankees were the first team to draw one million fans in a single season. They did so at the Polo Grounds owned by the Giants. Colonel Ruppert had offered $100,000 a year plus concession proceeds to the Giants. The Judge thought this a wonderful sum for what was, after all, as he put it, "the privilege of sharing the Polo Grounds with the Yankees." The Judge's view was that competition stopped at the foul line. John McGraw, amused at the thought of homeless rivals, rightly believed that there was no real estate left on the whole island of Manhattan big enough for another ballpark. McGraw's plan was simple. It fell into two parts. By part one, the Yankees were out of Manhattan. By part two, wherever they went, fans would not follow.

McGraw was wrong.

If Colonel Ruppert would build it, they would come.

The new Yankee Stadium went up across the Harlem River from the soon quaint-seeming old Polo Grounds.

The Judge had spoken of the trend in seeking to persuade McGraw: he pointed out periods during which the Yankees had outdrawn the Giants at the Polo Grounds. Yankees paying rent and increasing concession profits were a better spot for them to be than outside the Giants' control. But McGraw, his pride pricked, let them go. He had not listened to the Judge in 1921 and now, although not yet open, Yankee Stadium stood to overshadow his accomplishments. It would open in April 1923, surpassing Braves Field as the largest baseball stadium in the world, measured by surface area and crowd capacity.

But this was in the future. McGraw did not yet know how good the Judge's advice had been as he sat at his table in the Lambs Club. It was a characteristic contrast in their different personalities for McGraw to struggle for choke-holds on his competitors while the Judge espoused a gentlemanly code of good sportsmanship. One had grown up tough in baseball at its professional toughest; the other had grown up playing amateur ball at Maspeth Park. The two were deeply devoted to baseball, and admired one another, but they were different. The Judge was the contemplative fan, eager to recognize and root for the outstanding player, the outstanding play, the outstanding team. McGraw was congenitally unable to admire the other player, the other team, the baseball game outside his own reach, beyond his personal control. For the Judge the game was bigger than he was; for McGraw, he was bigger than the game.

It was only natural that McGraw interested himself in other teams and in their ownership. The trade or sale of players and of whole teams was capable of bending to his influence. It was also only natural that a team owner, fellow New Yorker George Washington Grant, should turn to McGraw to broker sale of his Boston Braves in late 1922. Grant, a cane-sporting, derby-wearing dandy who had made money on race horses, boxers and silent movie theaters in Europe, was losing money on the Braves. Having already sold stars like Nehf and McQuillan to McGraw and the great Rabbit Maranville to the Pirates, he had little left to sell but the team name itself. Could McGraw help?

McGraw could.

McGraw thought of the friend to whom he owed a team. Conscience-stricken, McGraw smarted on his throne. He had stolen his world champions out from under his friend's nose five years earlier. A hard-bitten sentimentalist when it came to old friends, McGraw saw in Grant's dilemma an opportunity for him to square things with that friend when both had seen acres of diamonds in the same team at the same time. The Giants had been the team, of course; the friend was George M. Cohan.

George M. Cohan the Giants fan and native New Englander might be inveigled into becoming a Braves owner, but it was going to be a tough sell. Like a spider spinning his web, McGraw began that autumn at the World Series, having his friend announced at the Polo Grounds to take a bow. But McGraw wanted Cohan to do more in baseball than take a bow. He wanted him to buy the Braves from Grant. Grant — drowning in red ink, in hock to bankers, having paid too much for the team, having sold his stars — had but the shell of a National League team left, the name and a lease on Braves Field. McGraw considered the situation. There would be no sense trying to compare teams.

The Giants had been the great money-machine, generating some $250,000 in profits most years. McGraw's (and what had been originally Cohan's) opportunity to buy the Giants had arisen under unusual conditions in 1918. That year was a war-shortened, player-short season in which no team in either league made money. However, the Giants were owned by somebody who did not want to own a ball team at all. While a chewing-gum magnate or a brewery lord would have had courage (and funds) to sit tight, the heirs of the estate of a money-losing ball club would not. Harry Hempstead, agent for his wife and mother-in-law, looked to sell the team, to turn their interest into income. He took offers under consideration, including an escalating series of bids by George M. Cohan, who had no problem telling his fellow Lambs what he was doing and how the bargaining was going. He felt that the ladies would come down to his top price eventually. Although the popular actor, director and producer — composer of over 500 songs, including "Over There," the best-selling hit west of the Western Front — was rich, he was also notoriously unwilling to pay more for anything than he had to.

McGraw, a poor man, his nose up against the glass of the candy-store, smelled money in baseball's comeback, but he had nothing, or almost nothing: he had picked up some information. He knew a good team was for sale, though not at a good price. Coming up late from behind, his contention unknown while newspapers ballyhooed Cohan's chase for the Giants, McGraw had had to chase money first. Only with a Tammany politician on one side of him and a wealthy casino owner on the other was he propped up financially enough to make an offer, a record-breaking offer. McGraw not only paid more for a team than anybody had ($1.3 million), he paid less than anybody ever had for a share. McGraw bought a $50,000 share for $338 in cash and a personal IOU for $49,662.

Cohan's slow talks with Hempstead stopped altogether with the surprise announcement. Cohan would have teetered between criticizing and congratulating McGraw. After all, he was already rich and Broadway offered many investment vehicles to a proven crowd-pleaser and judge of the tastes of the American public, while McGraw was broke and, besides, for him the deal represented more than money. For McGraw the Giants were the instrument of his immortality, the opportunity for one man to dominate the sport as none ever had. Moreover, had Cohan's initial impulse been critical, as the 1919 and 1920 seasons wallowed in the mud of the "Black Sox" scandal which threatened the ruin of anyone who had investments in baseball teams, Cohan would have mellowed into self-congratulation, having ducked risks he could not have foreseen and problems he might not have been able to solve. Baseball appeared to be coming apart at its seams as reporters and prosecutors throughout the country outraced one another to reconstruct and to reveal what had happened.

In baseball's darkest days the owners pulled the game out of its tailspin and hired a pilot to keep it on course. They probably thought that they were engaging a servant when they selected their new master, a federal judge from Chicago who had once conducted the Federal League's legal challenge to their monopoly through an erratic and finally stalled litigation schedule; the Federal League died a natural death before he had decided the matter. But the owners might have been surprised. And, if they expected accommodation when they hired their new commissioner — he told them the title of his office, what they were hiring him to be — they had sadly misjudged the judge. Kenesaw Mountain Landis, literally named after a Civil War battle, was a lively confrontationalist who soon took the name of the game as his own. Thereafter, his letterhead and stationery and his office door carried in bold, black letters the word "BASEBALL." Just "BASEBALL." And he was baseball. He made the rules, approved (or disapproved) the trades, investigated anything he wanted, summoned before him anyone he wanted, suspended players (some "for life"), heard appeals and would not himself be appealed. As part of his arrangement with the team owners, his word was final; should he direct litigation to be pulled, even litigation in some court by some team challenging his authority on something, they agreed to pull the litigation. He was judge and jury of anything that came up or anything he wanted to come up and anything he didn't want, didn't get done. Landis is blamed by many for maintaining the color line beyond its normal longevity. It is suggested that Branch Rickey had to wait until the Georgia-born son of a Confederate Army surgeon died before he could contract for the services of Jackie Robinson. But Landis's heritage includes much progress, some of which he achieved alone. For example, he negotiated World Series broadcast rights in 1934, initiating a whole new ball game financially, the ultimate foundation for astronomical salaries and league expansion.

Did Landis save baseball in his time?

The countercharge on scandal, some insist, was led not by Landis or owners and managers, but sluggers like Babe Ruth. John McGraw, however, was not among Ruth's early admirers. McGraw would not have taken Ruth in trade. McGraw did not want him; Ruth played the opposite of what McGraw thought constituted the game. For McGraw the game was won or lost by inches. His game was the right pitch, the timely bunt, the smart steal, expert fielding, all summed up in defense, careful control.

Bob Fuchs vouches for Babe Ruth's "control" game: he watched Babe Ruth entertain fans during spring training in St. Petersburg, where the Braves and the Yankees trained at Waterfront Park (now Al Lang Field). (Al Lang was given one year to live by his doctor so he retired to St. Petersburg and 20 years later enthusiastically introduced the major league teams to Florida.) Ruth placed two players, one at the plate and one alongside him at a second plate. And, with a ball in each hand threw a series of strikes to the batters simultaneously. But for Ruth — although Ruth had an enviable pitching record, right or left, and his fielding was about as perfect as earth allows — hitting was the game, and the home run baseball's reason to be. Ruth embodied the new game, the "lively ball," the "big bang" theory, a game not of inches but of hundreds of yards, a ball out of control, out of the park itself.

When McGraw first saw the future, he had said it would not work. Observing Ruth hit a 500-foot homer in Tampa during 1919 spring training, the then-new owner of the Giants said of the then-new Yankee, "If he plays every day, the bum will hit into a hundred double plays."

The showdown between the old and the new, between the game of inches and the game of yards, between the Giants and the Yankees, between McGraw and Ruth, began then and lasted until 1923. At first the old baseball showed strength. But, finally, new baseball prevailed. In 1921, 1922 and 1923 the best team of the National League was the Giants while the best of the American League was the Yankees. In each of those years the two pennant winners sailed into collision in a New York World Series, first in the park they shared, the Polo Grounds, where the hot dog had been invented in 1901 by Harry Stevens.

18 Judge Fuchs and the Boston Braves

(Bob Fuchs heard about it one balmy evening at the Judge's summer home in Belmar, New Jersey, on the upper porch overlooking the Shark River. The Judge's weekend guests became nostalgic, including a white-haired elderly man who reminisced saying, "Before the turn of the century I came over from England and worked as a cashier in a factory. A man came to pay his bill, threw his arms around me, recognizing me as a boyhood friend in England. After a chat he said, 'I've been successful since I came to the U.S. and if there is ever anything I can do for you don't hesitate to say so.' I replied, 'Yes, there is something I want to do, but I need $500 to get the business started.' My friend did not hesitate to lend me the money and I built a wooden tray with straps, purchased hot dogs, peanuts and soda, and went to Coogan's Bluff where I sold my wares. That was the start of Harry M. Stevens!")

But the Series, played entirely within the Polo Grounds in 1922, split like an amoeba in 1923. And the new life, "The House that Ruth Built," had the vitality of something new. The Yankees not only took the Series in 1923, they took the rest of the roaring twenties. The Giants were driven from the temple of champions. Ruth, up from his nadir mark of .117 in 1922, batted .368 in 19 plate appearances in 1923, including two singles, a double, a triple and three home runs. Personifying the new baseball, Ruth stood supreme, the little game of inches, the game of the inchworm John McGraw, dirt under his spiked shoes.

But when John McGraw invited George M. Cohan to lunch at the Lambs Club after the 1922 season, his Giants were the unbeaten and apparently unbeatable certified champions of the postwar world, and McGraw was the champion of champions and baseball was once again the Great American Game. McGraw, no longer a broke and broken-down player but a mover and a shaker, a hero and a celebrity drawing a salary higher than any manager ever besides making money out of the team he bought on time in time, greeted a fallen hero. Cohan, once the King of Broadway, had led the losing battle against Actors Equity in 1919, after which he dissolved his 15-year partnership with Sam Harris. The post office would say he lived in New Jersey but Cohan was actually living in the past, working not on musicals but on memoirs. Cohan, at lunch with show business and baseball people, the friend to whom "Muggsy" McGraw owed a baseball team, was being set up to buy the Boston Braves.

3

The Man Who Came to Dinner

"Baseball is my life — it has meant everything to me. If by chance, I get back on my feet, I have an ambition to revive the National League in Boston."

—Judge Fuchs, age 80, quoted in
The Sporting News (September 11, 1957)

McGraw had taken care to fill out the table with Cohan's friends. Old Sam Harris, William Farnum and Gene Buck were invited. Farnum, unlike Cohan who claimed the Fourth of July as his birthday but who had actually been born on July 3, was an actor born on the Fourth of July. Buck headed a Cohan-friendly union, the songwriter's guild. Producer-actor-songwriter Cohan sat among familiar friends from the Good Old Days.

McGraw brought George Washington Grant, Harry Stevens and Emil Fuchs. No doubt the richest of the baseball group assembled in the room, Stevens was the "hot dog king" whose rags-to-riches story decorated many Sunday supplements, a millionaire who demonstrated that a baseball dollar could be made in the stands as well as on the field. Because Stevens plied his wienies not only in New York with McGraw, but also in Boston with Grant, his presence was especially desired by McGraw since it was the Boston team that he wished Cohan to buy, hot dog franchise and all.

For Grant, who had sold the hot dog franchise to Stevens, who had been selling Braves player by player, the team he had bought in 1919 was a team on the way down. The 1914 world champs had touched each ladder rung by 1922: second (1915), third (1916), sixth (1917), seventh (1918), sixth (1919), fifth (1920), fourth (1921) and, completing its long and roller-coaster slide to the bottom of the National League, eighth team out of eight in

19

1922. Grant became what is known as a willing seller. He relied on the champion of champions, McGraw, to deliver the pitch.

The final member of the baseball quartet gathered at the Lambs Club by McGraw was Emil Fuchs. The Judge, who had known Cohan before Cohan produced his first hit, "Little Johnny Jones," in 1904, had achieved the title and nickname "Judge" from serving on the Magistrates Court from 1915 to 1918. Although McGraw retained the Judge as lawyer to defend the Giants and players in trouble, the Judge had many other clients. The history of New York had passed through his hands when he defended the election result for one governor. The now-wealthy Judge, who had drafted the contract by which control of the Giants went from Harry Hempstead to the trio of partners led by John McGraw in 1918, was at lunch as a living exhibit that there was money in baseball.

Things did not work out as planned.

McGraw, master strategist, was soon foiled in his effort to unload Grant's team on Cohan, whom McGraw might find useful as the owner of what some thought of as the Giants' "farm team."

After McGraw, no doubt quite consciously dropping the name of Cohan's most popular song, whispered, "That's George Washington Grant over there," and suggested a price only half of what he had paid for the Giants, some $650,000 for the Braves, Cohan had some fun.

Referring indirectly to 1918, Cohan reminded McGraw that it had been reported in the press that he was interested in or had bought every team in either league. But Cohan's only close pursuit of a team had been his negotiations with Harry Hempstead to buy the Giants, over which much ink was spilled over nothing. Cohan's criticism of his friend, so mute as to be unclear to any other listener, was succeeded by silliness unsurpassed in any play of his own devising.

"John, I'm a trouper," he said. "I'm a song and dance man. I love the theater. I was born of the theater and it looks as if I must stick to it until the final curtain."

This Byzantine and diplomatic rhetoric was words without substance. Cohan, divested of partnership, not only producing almost nothing, working on his memoirs, had developed into a virtual recluse. Had he said that he was retired or that he was going to Europe he would have made sense. But for him to say there was no business like show business was superb irony. Although he would stage something of a comeback beginning in 1925, no commitment or active tie to the theater beckoned him with the least distraction from investing time or money in the Braves in 1922.

In classic theatrical tradition, Cohan invited the spotlight to another.

Tossing back the "over there" phrase to McGraw, he asked, "How about our old friend over there, Judge Fuchs?"

Before allowing the Judge an opportunity to stand and deliver a speech about being a lawyer, an advocate who loved the court, who wooed every jury with pleasure and who seemed destined to stick to it until the last pound of the gavel, Cohan threw in a sweetener that was music to McGraw's ears.

"He's the greatest baseball fan I know of in New York. He never misses a chance to go to a ball game. If he'll buy the team, I'll buy some stock."

For McGraw the multiplying possibilities of both Cohan and his lawyer buying the Braves and the continuation of that team in Giants-friendly hands, while doing Grant a timely favor, had to have quickened his pulse. But he said nothing. It was up to the Judge to reply. And the Judge left it up to Christy Mathewson.

"John, I'll tell you what I'll do," the Judge said. "One of my idols and friends is Christy Mathewson, in whom I have not only admiration but every confidence. I'd buy the Braves if I could continue my law practice and he'd be general manager and president."

McGraw's pulse probably shot up to a hundred beats a minute on that suggestion. From Cohan to the Judge to Mathewson, and with Mathewson, the Giants legend, in charge of it all, underwritten by two wealthy baseball fans in New York...

The Judge, like Cohan, distinguished between investing and actively running a ball club but, unlike Cohan, for the Judge distractions were real. Middle-aged, a lawyer married with children, running an established and busy solo practice that had made him rich, the Judge loved the city in which he had grown up and thrived. The Judge was willing to be one of the Braves' temporary absentee owners provided there was somebody competent really in charge protecting his investment. When the bottom-rung team was in a better state, the team would be sold at a profit or — and the Judge hoped for it — sold at cost to a reinvigorated Mathewson. It was a team that "needs work" more than mere money.

But Mathewson was a highly unlikely partner. Although many fans would have gladly voted for Mathewson over Warren Harding for president and, similarly, his nomination for president of any ball club would have been by acclamation, Mathewson had not been active in baseball for a good long time. Indeed, he had not been very active at all. Afflicted by tuberculosis that had been aggravated during combat duty "Over There," Mathewson lived quietly 300 miles north of the Manhattan club where gentlemen talked over tinkling glasses about the possibility of Big Six coming back to baseball. It was known that Mathewson could and did walk about, that he had mastered chess and was an expert in checkers, in which he could play several games simultaneously, and he played major league auction bridge. McGraw, who kept in touch with his former star by long distance phone calls every month or so, got the operator to bring them into connection with a cottage in Saranac Lake and, when Mathewson answered, turned the phone over to the Judge.

The Judge explained without making any attempt to persuade. A return to baseball was offered, in management, with the Boston Braves. A return to baseball with the National League's worst team at the team's worst time, changing ownership, losing players. The Judge could and would raise the dough if—and only if—Mathewson would run the team. Mathewson agreed to call back in an hour.

During that hour the show business people disappeared, leaving the baseball people together. The Judge, who thought McGraw a master of baseball, may have sought McGraw's opinion of the wisdom of the purchase. The Judge had previously, in a smaller way, put his money where John McGraw's mouth was. Once, $500 of the Judge's money had ridden on McGraw's judgment. Giants co-owner and astute bettor Charlie Stoneham had come up to McGraw's office upstairs in back of center field at the Polo Grounds asking whether the master had looked at the day's batting order. Stoneham pointed out that McGraw had a lefty pitching to nine right-hand hitters. The Judge, upon McGraw's insistence that the southpaw pitch, bet Stoneham $500 on the game, the Giants to win. Art Nehf (acquired from the Boston Braves) proceeded not only to win but also to shut out the entire batting order.

McGraw was not so respectful of the Judge's advice in turn, and sometimes it cost him. The Judge, who had had to put pitcher Jesse Barnes on the witness stand for a miserable morning of cross examination, gave him a note for McGraw. "Dear John," it read, "I understand it is Jesse's turn to pitch today. I respectfully suggest you don't do it." When court recessed for the day, the Judge, following his custom, hustled out to the Polo Grounds. He beheld simultaneously Jesse Barnes on the mound and 10 runs on the scoreboard, the first half of the first inning not over yet. The Judge never recorded whether McGraw acknowledged his lawyer's insight or apologized.

Another apology to which the Judge probably could lay claim, but never seems to have received, was one from the commissioner. Landis, after the trial in which Jesse Barnes testified, the criminal prosecution of Benny Kauff for stealing cars, used the prerogative he had arranged with team owners not to be the subject of litigation challenging or appealing his rulings.

At trial, witnesses including Jesse Barnes, John McGraw and baseball celebrities testified, often only as to character. The Judge put Governor John Tanner of Pennsylvania (later president of the National League) through questions that assisted the jury reach the conclusion to acquit Kauff. Tanner testified, "When I was governor of Pennsylvania, I reviewed the boys that were going over there to fight the war for Uncle Sam, and among those I greeted and bade farewell was the defendant, Benny Kauff, in uniform."

Character witnesses and celebrities apart, a noncharacter noncelebrity witness named Schwartz proved the case for the defense: according to Schwartz — allegedly the victim of theft according to the prosecution — he had sold his car to Kauff.

Kauff's trial, Act One, followed by his acquittal, Act Two, led to Act Three, baseball commissioner Landis's suspension of the player from the Giants' roster.

The Judge went to court. Given a jury verdict of innocence against Landis's opinion (from reading a transcript of testimony at trial), the Judge felt sure that a judge would enforce the verdict over the opinion and reinstate Kauff to earn an honest living in New York. Only as the Judge was arguing this point before the New York Supreme Court did Landis act, playing his trump, ordering the Giants to order their lawyer to withdraw the case for Kauff's reinstatement. Case closed.

Landis's self-serving declaration that the transcript he had read made him believe that the Kauff acquittal was "one of the worst miscarriages of justice ever brought to (his) attention," had to have particularly stung the Judge, Kauff's lawyer. It may have been exhilarating at least in a minor key for the Judge to imagine, as owner of the Braves, having some power over his recent vocal critic and trump-card player.

But the Judge, keeping any exhilaration on a short leash, bided his time for an hour without commenting on Landis.

Mathewson called back.

"I have decided," he said, but the great pitcher had only decided to come to New York, something he had not done since launching a campaign for contributions to fight TB the year before. He would meet the Judge at the quiet Hotel Bretton Hall, a family establishment where his arrival might escape notice. Nobody wanted publicity over something not settled. Shades of Cohan's 1918 negotiations!

The next day Mathewson met the Judge at the hotel and told him, "I have given every thought to this since our talk over the long distance telephone. I spoke to my good wife, Jane, about it. She advised against it at the beginning of our talk, but finally said, 'Matty, if it's your desire to go back to the game of your youth and affection, go ahead.' Judge, I would rather spend another two or three years in the only occupation and vocation I know than to linger many years up in Saranac Lake."

The Judge, no doubt as amazed as anyone else that he should be responsible for Christy Mathewson's return to the game, amazed to find himself purchaser of a major league team, immediately laid out a plan to invest and divest. His law firm came first. Although he would raise the money, most of it his own, he wanted none from Mathewson. If things went well, Mathewson could buy the Judge out at the original purchase price, or as much of the Judge's interest as he wished. The Judge only sought to break even. He hoped that Mathewson's health would permit him to set the Boston Braves on track for success; indeed, Mathewson's health was a key factor planned on. The Judge anticipated that Mathewson would rebound upon his return, putting it this way in his memoirs: "The thought struck me that perhaps if he were actively connected with baseball again that the environment he loved might give him an added incentive to fight his way back to health. That alone would justify my entrance to baseball."

The Judge always remained glad about the advice he gave to Mathewson against investing in the Braves.

"I told him not to assume any financial burden. The opportunity would always be there at the original price if the club were successful. I was always glad I did not permit him to assume that additional worry."

The Judge "talked terms" with Grant, obtaining the team for $350,000. Grant sold at a loss. For $50,000 down, the Judge obtained and took a couple of months to raise the rest, with other New Yorkers including banker James McDonough. With the balance the Judge and Mathewson took a train from New York to Boston in February 1923, paying Grant at Braves Field and hosting a press conference the same day at the Copley Plaza.

Newsboys screamed headlines of Christy Mathewson once more. Mathewson told reporters that he tipped the scales at 204 pounds, had never weighed more and felt that "next to managing, it's the most fun of all to be president of a ball club." George M. Cohan, wherever he was that day, the friend from whom John McGraw had poached a ball club, savored materials for a play he never wrote (although he did produce a baseball play in 1928, *Elmer the Great*). That theatrical genius, who directed and produced a role for the Judge in American baseball, the fan-becomes-owner, could not have known that it was the beginning of a 12-year riches-to-rags tragedy, but he would have recalled the lunch at the Lambs Club when the prospective buyer convinced the seller's agent's lawyer to buy a ball club, so that the Judge (instead of Cohan) became the man who came to dinner. And the Judge, on an impulse to allow Christy Mathewson's baseball career extra innings, found himself owner of the Boston Braves in 1923, an ownership which would continue until 1935.

George Washington Grant, in a farewell anticipating by many years the remarks by Lou Gehrig in Yankee Stadium, said, "If the people of Boston that I have met think as much of me as I do of them, I should be the happiest man in the world."

4

The Braves of Boston

"The wrong fellow sold his ball club."
— Bostonians' consensus, contrasting
George Washington Grant against
Harry Frazee, New York *Telegram* (1923)

Braves Field was built as James Gaffney's way out of baseball. He built the field and then disposed of his team, evolving from owner to landlord in the process. Gaffney knew when to buy and when to sell. In 1912, Gaffney, a "Tammany Tiger," had jumped a line of bankers and the sports entrepreneur George Washington Grant to pay the heirs of a New York lawyer $187,000 for the team. The team got a new name as the "Braves" owned by this Tammany "Chief." The team followed him to an unequaled thrill a season later, shooting up from last place to first in their league in ten weeks, then taking the Series in four straight games. Sensing an end to miracles and hearing guns booming in Europe, Gaffney unloaded his tribe on bankers for some $300,000 in 1916 and the bankers sold to George Washington Grant for $400,000 in 1919. The sale to the Judge and Mathewson in 1923 was the fifth to a New Yorker or New York partnership. Gaffney, who had shoveled out $450,000 to turn a riverside golf course and swamp into a green cathedral, had seen them come and seen them go. He and his heirs held a 30-year lease by which they had spooned back $45,000 a year, while the team picked up the real estate taxes. In fact, the lease he had signed with himself before he sold his team would return over $1 million to him and his family. But, for the Braves, the field he had built was a bad dream.

Gaffney had built a monumental stadium, the largest baseball field in the world until Yankee Stadium was built almost ten years later. The covered bleachers were so solid that they could be used as a foundation for a second story. (Press boxes *were* placed on those 30-year-old roofs to cover the 1946 season.) The Braves' locker room was so large that, when Boston University took the property over in the 1950s, all of its four athletic teams outfitted and stored equipment in the spacious facility. There was room in the external fencing for a second gate (nearer the Charles River) if expansion later proved justified. It never was. The outfield was so large that an 8,000-fan "jury box" was constructed to face center field during the Judge's time, without much increasing the total of home runs hit out of the park. Ty Cobb had predicted nobody would ever hit a ball out of Braves Field. His prediction held good for five years and was not often contradicted in games even after the "jury box" was built.

The truth is, the golf-course-swamp-turned-into-a-ball-park was built in 1914, another era, for another era. It was intended to be the perfect park for the controlled-ball "game of inches" epitomized by John McGraw and which, in 1923, suffered ignominious defeat. The walls and fences of Braves Field were purposely distant, out of the best batter's reach. McGraw's 1923 defeat was handwriting on Braves Field's walls.

Although between 1914 and 1921 the bunt-and-steal Giants rose from last to first place in the National League, using these hitless tactics as their entire strategy the Braves between 1914 and 1922, slid from first to last in the same league. The only home runs intended in Boston were the inside-the-park variety. Stranded in Braves Field, Boston's National Leaguers were isolated from the type of parks and environment enjoyed by mainstream players in 1923.

The Judge and team president Mathewson, tutored by John McGraw, came out of the old ball game. Mathewson had produced his results as a control pitcher with precision fielding. The Braves were in Boston while the revolution was taking place, as the old house of baseball was being dismantled and replaced by many mansions of the House that Ruth Built. Until the Braves moved out of Braves Field to Milwaukee the greatest of the Braves were pitchers and fielders. Braves came to be known by such players as Hank Aaron decades after and ball parks removed from Braves Field at 1923. Playing old-fashioned, conservative, not-to-lose baseball during the Ruthian revolution, the Braves stalled throughout the twenties. It characterizes the Braves of 1923 that the great event of that season was shortstop Ernie Padgett's unassisted triple play during their last game, October 6, 1923.

Padgett barely attained that feat; he'd been in the majors only ten days and was playing his first full game. The game (second half of a double-header) was begun so late in the day — after a 14-inning duel between

Philadelphia and Boston over who would be the cellar team of the National League, which Boston won 5-to-4 — was agreed to last five innings. Padgett's play ended the fourth inning; Boston won 4-to-1.

The Boston Braves in 1923 did offer passing views of other historic feats, however. For example, on September 20, 1923, at Braves Field in the first game of a doubleheader Ty Cobb had four hits in four at-bats to establish a new benchmark in lifetime hits. Honus Wagner's 3,430 hits record (during a 21-year career) faded before Cobb's performance, achieved within 19 years.

Road trips always provided a welcome change. The Braves traveled well. The team never won more than half its games at home, although it won exactly half its home games in 1934, the only season that it did so during the years the Judge owned the team. But the team won better than five out of ten away games in 1926, 1930, 1932, 1933 and 1934, and the team did better on the road every season except the first year, 1923, when it was worse on the road than it was in any season, winning fewer than three out of ten away games.

The net result of the Braves Field handicap and a hitting void within the team explains the twenties, when the team finished seventh (1923), eighth (1924), fifth (1925), seventh (1926), seventh (1927), seventh (1928) and eighth (1929). Not until a combination of players including Rookie of the Year Wally Berger, whose ability to hit home runs developed early, and still limping at home but walking on the road, did the Braves in the thirties play .500 ball, and even end in the First Division, having flirted with the National League pennant.

In 1923 the best was yet to come. In 1923 the team that "needed work," needed work. And the Judge found that his partner was not only not cured, he was not well. Christy Mathewson, known as "Big Six," who had towered on the mound as a literal giant, was in the grips of a breath-stealing killer. He met every scheduled commitment, but it was grueling and required virtual commuting between Saranac Lake and Boston, between recuperation and responsibilities. The Judge found himself shuttling by train from his New York law office to the Copley Plaza Hotel in Boston, also virtually a commuter.

One can visualize the situation. The Judge, whose reason to become owner of the Braves derived from Mathewson's return to baseball, would not do anything to reduce that role. Mathewson, a man of honor who had

Opposite: **Braves Field, Boston, Massachusetts, opening day 1930 (courtesy of the Boston Braves Historical Association).**

decided that he would go down swinging, consciously aware that his return would shorten his life, minimized his difficulties. Only his wife and doctor ever heard him speak frankly about his condition. Accordingly, the Judge had to enjoy the ride more than require that it bring him somewhere in particular, such as the World Series. From Jim Gaffney they were saddled with Braves Field. When George Washington Grant conceded to sell at their price, he required that they continue his manager, Fred Mitchell, in employment. Though they eventually replaced Mitchell with Dave "Beauty" Bancroft of Harvard athletic fame, Mitchell remained chief of scouts on a one-scout team without having to reduce his standard of living or headquarters.

The Judge himself made no habit of worry or of complaint. With a lucrative law practice until the Depression, he indulged himself with baseball — and bridge, in which he was an expert and an addict. Bridge games on wheels (by cab, train and cab again) left New York and arrived in Boston with him. Once at his Boston hotel he would continue to play bridge, looking for his partner, Christy Mathewson. Mathewson, from long years of practice at Saranac Lake, played like a champion. It was further a tic with him to instruct others. The Boston *Globe*'s baseball columnist, Uncle Jim O'Leary, something of a character with cigar ashes all over his bulging vest, was Mathewson's constant pupil. The pitcher would patiently pry one of the columnist's hands away from the cards, but O'Leary, sooner or later, would automatically resume his two handed grip and there would be another lesson from the master.

The Judge enjoyed reporters' company and worked to raise spirits through the annual losing seasons with choruses of songs, including the one popularized on stage by George M. Cohan, "Take Me Out to the Ball Game." Attending and running dinners and men-only smokers, the Judge was more popular than the song and developed a reputation for grabbing checks as he passed through restaurants greeting friends, acquaintances and hangers-on. Through it all, beginning with his first year, he felt amply repaid by Mathewson's participation in the sport he loved, and by the atmosphere, the characters who fascinated him, so different from his round of office consultations, jury trials and court appeals in New York. Beyond mere colorful characters, as a fan he looked in awe on the great players, hobnobbed cheerfully now as an owner among other owners, absorbing what he saw and heard for later telling and retelling.

At a 1923 spring training exhibition game he witnessed Steve McKeever, who thereafter became a lead character in his repertoire of stories. McKeever, whose baseball interest began late in life when he traded construction of Ebbets Field for stock in the Dodgers, was supposed to have run away at age 11 to join the Union Army as a drummer boy, but the army would not have him for one reason or another. McKeever in his own time enlisted in Abner Doubleday's latter-day uniformed army of baseball players; he was a man who simply loved to march, loved a parade, even at a ball park.

As the Judge recalled and reported it:

> A new practice field of the Dodgers was to be dedicated in Clearwater, Florida in the spring of 1923. It was to be a gala occasion with the Chamber of Commerce planning a program that began with a band concert and speeches, and was to be concluded with a banquet in the cool of the evening.
>
> The Dodgers were scheduled to play an exhibition game that afternoon with the Phillies. One of the exercises planned was a march to the flagpole by the players of both clubs, led by the band.
>
> Someone, probably connected with the Brooklyn club, canceled the parade in order to keep McKeever from marching. There was something of a mystery about it, but anyhow the Brooklyn players were told that they were not to march.
>
> McKeever was disappointed deeply when he heard the parade had been called off. He was not discouraged, however, because he was determined to have the parade anyhow.
>
> He went over to the Philadelphia bench and addressed the visiting players, "The show must go on," he said. "The fans came here this afternoon to see a parade and we're going to give them one. Line up, boys, we're going to march out to the flagpole."
>
> The Phillies, who probably loved a parade too, were a little bit puzzled by the turn of events but they lined up and, headed by McKeever and the band, marched out to the flagpole. After the flag was raised McKeever said, "Wait a minute, boys, I have something I want to discuss with you.
>
> "Now, gentlemen," he continued, "the Brooklyn club has bought a shortstop named Raymond French for $30,000. French refuses to sign a Brooklyn contract or report to the club until he receives $5,000 more than his contract calls for.
>
> "I argued the matter with the board of directors of the Brooklyn club, saying that after paying $30,000 for French, what good is he to us unless he plays. So I will put this question up for a vote before this impartial assemblage. All those in favor of French getting the $5,000 will respond in the customary manner."
>
> The Phillies in one loud chorus shouted, "Aye, give French the $5,000."
>
> "Contrary-minded?" queried McKeever.
>
> There was not a peep.
>
> "Unanimously carried. So ordered. So recorded. I congratulate you, gentlemen, on your verdict," responded McKeever.
>
> Then he lined up the Phillies in single file and headed the procession back to the grandstand where he announced the decision to President Ebbets and manager Wilbert Robinson.
>
> Needless to say, French received his request for the increase and became a member in good standing of the Brooklyn club.

The Judge reveled in this new world, or old world seen more from an insider's perspective than ever. He became something of a baseball character himself in time, once deputizing Ring Lardner to sit as judge between the aforementioned Dodgers' Wilbert Robinson and himself over a dispute they had concerning the value of a trade. The Braves traded pitcher Jesse Barnes — the same pitcher put on the mound once by John McGraw after a bumbling morning on the witness stand — outfielder Gus Felix and catcher Mickey O'Neil to Brooklyn for outfielder Ed Brown, infielders Andy High and Jimmy Johnston and catcher Zack Taylor. According to the Judge:

> Robby was convinced that he had gotten the better of the deal after it was made and I, of course, felt that we had improved our club considerably. Many of the baseball writers were in our quarters at the Hotel Schenley in Pittsburgh where we were attending the World Series.
> They were taking sides and it seemed that the score was about even as to which club had benefited most by the trade. Finally it was suggested that we put it up to Lardner to decide.
> Lardner agreed to be the arbiter. He reviewed the players who had been involved and finally said, "After considering the evidence presented it is my opinion that you both got stuck."

Lardner's judgment was not the only judgment the new owner valued, or was his effort to obtain advice and help without an amusing side, which he later recorded making some speakers anonymous:

> Three major league managers and two managers of minor league clubs were seated in the room of a new major league owner at a hotel during a minor league meeting.
> During a lull in the conversation which, naturally, was all about the national pastime, the new major league owner said, "Gentlemen, tell me something more about that unselfish gentleman, Branch Rickey, who so kindly has volunteered to help me build a championship club, despite the fact that we are rivals in the same league."
> The first major league manager asked, "Did Branch start the conversation by saying, 'You are a new man in the National League and your city has not had a pennant in 10 years or more, so I will now give you the benefit of my experience, try to help you and forget that my entire allegiance should be to the St. Louis Cardinals. I will put myself in your shoes and become your chief scout and manager. What you — I might say, what WE need — are five starting pitchers. They must be smart, have a fast ball that hops, a good change of pace, and a slow ball that tries the patience of the hitter.
> 'We must realize that no club can win steadily unless it is fortified right down the middle, from catcher, through the pitcher's box to center field with a fine double play combination around second base. Those ten good men will be the backbone of our ball club?'"

The new major league owner, answering, said, "Yes, that is just what he said. He was good enough to tell me all of that in confidence."

"Was he kind enough to offer these stars to you?" asked the second major league manager.

"I should not have violated his confidence," replied the new major league owner, "but he said he would use his influence with Sam Breadon to see if he would sell me some of his major and minor league stars in order to help me."

Then the third major league manager stepped up to bat and said, "Let me tell you about a high pressure salesman who became despondent because things were not breaking well and was determined to end it all. He decided to take a header off the Brooklyn Bridge and was getting ready to take the plunge when a cop came along. Rushing over, the cop reached the high pressure salesman just in time and pulled him back. Both stood arguing for about ten minutes, with the high pressure salesman having the floor most of the time."

"What happened?" breathlessly asked the new major league owner.

"Why, they both got up on the railing and took the dive together," was the response.

"Who was the salesman?" asked the new owner.

"Why, he was one of Branch Rickey's pupils," was the answer.

Evidently not impressed by the moral of the story, the new owner said, "Well, gentlemen, I am indeed fortunate to have gained the confidence of such a good friend and advisor in my first year in the National League."

Turning to the minor league managers, the new owner asked, "Are you gentlemen fortunate enough to know this great man?"

The first minor league manager answered, "Yes, indeed, we run farms for him and have done so for 17 years. You deserve congratulations for being able to win the pennant next season."

Then the second minor league manager said, "And may I add that when Mr. Rickey gets to know you better he also might be persuaded to sell you our great first and third basemen, also a couple of outfielders to complete your team."

The new owner said, "Thank you, gentlemen, and may I propose a silent toast to the poor Cardinals and Yankees this coming season."

What they toasted with in 1923, with prohibition not ending for another decade, is not recorded. But it is recorded that in 1924, the next season, the Braves finished in last place of the eight teams in the National League.

It was during these early years that Hall of Famer (1971) Richard "Rube" Marquard pitched for the Braves (1922 through 1925) and then served as a coach.

At 16, against his father's orders, Marquard hopped a freight train from Cleveland to Waterloo, in the Iowa State League, for five days with just enough money for three days' food. Management wouldn't even advance him $5 for food! Exhausted from his five-day bumming, he was told to pitch the next day — and won 6–1. But even then management wouldn't advance

Champion golfer Walter Hagen, businessman Jack Taylor, Judge Fuchs and winner of 19 straight games, Rube Marquard, at spring training in St. Petersburg, Florida, in 1925 (from the Robert S. Fuchs Collection).

him $5 until he again pitched against a more formidable team. Rube (he acquired his nickname, not because he was considered a country boy, but because someone said he looked like the great Rube Waddell) went back to Cleveland via freight route rather than be taken advantage of. En route he found warmth in an empty firehouse where he was found sound asleep by the returning firemen. Learning that he had not eaten for days the firemen passed the hat and gave him about $5. He promised he would some day come back to visit them when he was in Chicago in the big leagues — and he kept his promise, making the firehouse his headquarters when the Giants were in Chicago — to the delight of the firemen, their families, and all of the kids in the neighborhood. A rookie in Indianapolis, he was laughed at when he pitched an exhibition game against Cleveland, asking him if he was the bat boy — but facing Napoleon Lajoie, Terry Turner, Elmer Flick, George Stovel and the others for whom he had carried bats as a youth, he shut them out 2–0.

When Cleveland offered $3,500 for his contract Rube was insulted and said he would rather go back to the ice cream company back home. Following a great year, the team played in Columbus, Ohio. Both major league teams had an off day, so scouts watched the game. Marquard faced 27 batters and no one reached first base. This led to an auction which was won by the Giants who paid the most ever for a minor league player — $11,000.

Marquard never drank or smoked. Ten years after his leaving home his father came to a game as his first sign that he forgave his son for becoming a ball player.

A Boston Braves coach also in the twenties had long been a Boston Brave, Hank Gowdy.

In 1914, the year of the "Miracle Braves," his batting average was .243 — but come the World Series he hit the jackpot. Gowdy, who played in only 49 games between 1923 and 1926 for the Braves, in the 1914 World Series was unstoppable. He batted .545 and hit the only home run of the games. Five of his six hits were for extra bases and as a result of his streak he drew five walks in the Series.

Later, Gowdy was the first major leaguer to enlist in the Army in World War I. He was in the same regiment with and close friend of Joyce Kilmer, the author of *Trees*.

Reminiscing about his war-time experiences, Gowdy told an eerie story of being in a foxhole when his platoon was ordered to advance. However, the barrage of German guns forced a retreat and he returned to the same foxhole where, to his amazement, a bomb had landed in his absence — and, looking at a piece of the bomb he was awestruck to read the serial number: some seven numbers identical to his own serial number!

When Gowdy returned from the Army he was recognized as the first player to enlist in the service. Home in Columbus, Ohio, he received numerous invitations to speak. Recognizing Gowdy's nervousness his host advised him to pick out someone in the audience who did not look too prepossessing and speak to him. Gowdy followed his advice, targeting a rather elderly man who had a large trumpet-like hearing aid in his left ear. The speech went well and Gowdy thanked his host for the advice. Pointing out the gentleman in the audience with the hearing aid, Gowdy asked his host if he knew him. His host replied, "Of course, that's Thomas Edison!"

The Judge recalled Bill Klem of the early twenties. As the Judge told it:

> Klem, one of the greatest umpires who ever pulled on a mask, was officiating at a game at Braves Field. Ross Young, brilliant young outfielder of the Giants, had tried to steal second but the catcher's throw was in time in Dave Bancroft's glove, so Klem called him out.
>
> Young immediately protested vigorously. "He never touched me," shouted Young, "he missed me by a foot."
>
> "That's what they all say. I never miss the call," responded Klem. "You're out!"

"Go have your eyes examined and then retire," advised the fuming Young.

"You retire and take a shower for yourself," ordered the exploding Klem.

"No wonder base stealing is becoming a lost art, but larceny still is with us," was the final retort of the player as he strolled off the field.

The Braves were scheduled to play in New York the next day, so we caught the 6 o'clock train. Christy Mathewson, Bancroft and I were sitting in a drawing room when Klem walked by. Someone suggested a bridge game, and everyone was willing. I drew Banny, and Matty and Klem were partners.

Banny and I won about seven dollars and Matty said to Klem, "You pay Banny, Bill, the Judge and I have a running account and I'll settle with him."

Banny started to kid Klem and said, "Never mind about paying me, Bill, just give me a close one once in a while, like you did today, and I'll call it even."

"There *are* no close ones," responded Klem. "They either are out or they are safe. There is no such thing as a close one, and as I said to Young today, I never miss them."

"Well, you missed that one," replied Banny.

"Never missed one in my life," responded Klem.

Banny told Klem about coming up to the New York club from Philadelphia.

Duffy Lewis, Zack Taylor, Judge Fuchs, Bill McKechnie and Hank Gowdy, members of the "Miracle Braves" of 1914, are pictured in 1926 at spring training in St. Petersburg, Florida (from the Robert S. Fuchs Collection).

"I was walking to my position the first day when Frank Snyder the catcher said I now was with a smart ball club, and that I should know the signs. I told him that I had known the Giants' signs all season. That's why the Giants paid Philadelphia $105,000 for my contract."

"What's that got to do with your saying I missed one this afternoon?" Klem insisted.

"Well," said Banny, "the day I played my first game against the Pirates Honus Wagner was stealing second base. I took the throw from the catcher and put it on Wagner's foot as he slid feet first into the bag. The shock knocked the ball out of my hand, and the umpire, who had called Wagner out, now reversed and called him safe.

"During fielding practice the next day Wagner, who seemed to take an interest in me, came over and said 'Young fellow, let me give you a little advice and if you follow it, what happened yesterday will not happen again.

"'Never touch the runner with the ball. Just make a bluff of touching him by coming close. Never actually *touch* him. Always pull your hand away and hold up the ball to the umpire as if you had made the touch. Then see what happens.'

"That happened ten years ago, Bill. I never have touched a runner since that day in Pittsburgh, and I never have lost a decision."

"You're just bragging," was all Klem said.

The Braves were playing the Giants the next afternoon at the Polo Grounds.

Fred Lindstrom, the Giants' third sacker, was on first base. Klem was umpiring on the bases. Lindstrom started to steal second. The catcher's throw was fast and accurate. Banny had it before Lindstrom arrived.

This is how Banny told it that afternoon: "I remember what I had told Klem the night before, and I knew he would be looking for something. So for the first time in ten years I put the ball squarely on the runner at least five feet before he reached the bag."

"Safe," declared Klem.

"What do you mean, Bill?" I said. "You know I had him by at least five feet."

"But you didn't touch him!" responded Bill. "Don't you remember, you told me yesterday you never touch them?"

"It served me right for ever confiding in an umpire. I learned my lesson. I'll never brag again."

5

Christy Mathewson's Last Hurrah

"It may require some little time to obtain winning results."
— Christy Mathewson (1923)

It was 1919. It was a "brave new world" year. The war was over and anything and everything seemed possible. "Over There" the guns were silent. Diplomats in Paris met to work out the peace. They drew a new map over old Europe. They set in place a League of Nations to keep the peace and preserve the world they made. Gamblers in New York met to fix the World Series. They cast a net to catch as many players of the first-rated Chicago White Sox as they could. Editors met in New York to put together their World Series staffs. The *New York World*, Pulitzer's paper, scored a coup. The *World* hired Christy Mathewson to cover the World Series.

Mathewson, although known as a pitcher, was a published author. A college graduate who possessed a keen mind and terrific memory, Mathewson was seen as the ideal person to bridge the gap between the players and the public, to observe and to articulate what was happening on the field every day. So it was that the author of *Pitching in a Pinch* and the novel *Second Base Sloan* (which Bob Fuchs read as a child and thoroughly enjoyed) registered at the Sinton Hotel in Cincinnati to share a room with Chicago columnist Hugh Fullerton. Fullerton, a capable enough sports reporter, surprised Mathewson by suggesting they team up. Fullerton explained that he had heard rumors that the Series was fixed, that the Chicago team was to lose.

Mathewson wanted to know how he could help Fullerton.

Fullerton was sure that Mathewson's keen eyes could detect baseball impurities that would escape the notice of thousands of intently-watching fans. Given the circumstances of the World Series, Fullerton was convinced that the "muffed" plays would be of the most undetectable kind. Indeed, he thought — rightly — that the White Sox would not lose four games straight.

Some combination of professional pride and a concept of duty led Mathewson to pledge his gift of sight the next few days to the use of Hugh Fullerton. He, the baseball "insider," his livelihood even as an author dependent upon the game, was willing to pull down the house of baseball and put his word and his credibility on the line against people he had known and worked with for decades, if it came to that. He agreed to "spot" suspicious plays, creating a record of these evanescent events simultaneously within each game. He would signal to Fullerton with a gesture; Fullerton would make a note on his scorecard. Otherwise, both went on about the business of covering the Series.

Neither Fullerton nor Mathewson (nor any other writer) reported a "fix" during the Series. The story could not be imagined unless Cincinnati won and, even after that, not until courts specified charges, named names and identified the plays which, in a pattern, constituted a conspiracy against fair play. Mathewson literally saw over the heads of the crowd of screaming fans. Fullerton ultimately reported not what he had seen but what Christy Mathewson had seen. Mathewson's evidence was the most credible proof possible that there had been something wrong with the 1919 Series.

But for Mathewson's "pointers" to Fullerton, professional baseball might have declined into a sort of gaudy sideshow, with the same public impression which (rightly or wrongly) is associated with horse racing and professional wrestling. Dishonest sports are simply not popular. The game which is thought to be rigged is watched, at best, as entertainment, warily and unenthusiastically. Given a game in which the most intently-watched and public spectacle of all, the Series, could be undetectably rigged, fans would have deserted. But given a sport in which crime does not pay, in which sharp eyes police the field for the least suspicious goof or compromise, Americans would fill the bleachers still. Mathewson asserted not one but two things: first, that a baseball fix was, indeed, detectable; and, only second, that the 1919 Series had been a scandal. It was far less important whether or not the 1919 games and plays represented a fix — to this day partisans insist that some players, at least, of the "eight men out" were innocent — than that baseball could be played honestly and blemishes would always be apparent. This point made, baseball was safe. It was, then and thus, that Christy Mathewson and not Babe Ruth or Commissioner Kenesaw Mountain Landis saved the great American game.

Before he saved the sport, before he enlisted in a two-reporter army of conscience, Mathewson was his own man, and a master of control. No pitcher of either league ever pitched more 20-win seasons than Christy Mathewson. Mathewson's ball went where he wanted it to go. Mathewson's ability to pitch increased. During his thirteenth 20-win season in 1914 he pitched an unprecedented streak of 12 consecutive victories. This on-the-mound control mirrored his life off the field. He never drank, smoked nor swore. He played chess, checkers and bridge until he was a world class expert at all three. Mathewson's mother knew him best. When she came to die, she exercised the deathbed privilege of asking her son to promise her something. Of all the promises she might have asked, it is obvious that she knew of only one way Christy Mathewson would ever be tempted to break any of the Ten Commandments. She asked for and received his promise that he would never pitch on Sundays.

Mathewson never did pitch on Sundays. But he interpreted his promise to his mother quite literally. On Sunday, August 19, 1917, Mathewson, manager for the Cincinnati Reds, played against John McGraw, manager for the New York Giants, at the Polo Grounds in a game held for the benefit of the Army. Summoned before the Magistrates Court, Mathewson and McGraw, both guilty of Sabbath-breaking, were free to go as soon as the charges were dismissed by a sympathetic and patriotic judge. Mathewson soon after left for his stint of wartime service, leading a group in chemical warfare. Repeated exposure to poisonous gas during training damaged his lungs. Within a few years Mathewson, an incipient tuberculosis rising to full force within his body, lay low with a life-threatening illness.

Ill or well, Mathewson was an attractive prospect to preside over a major league team only to an owner committed to fair play. Owners, including John McGraw, who had established a federal judge to police their teams at large, did not necessarily want such a man at every game watching every play. Although, for Judge Fuchs, Mathewson was not his first choice but his only choice of partner, for other owners Mathewson was no choice at all. But where others saw a crippled gadfly, the Judge saw a man of honor, the personification of baseball's most precious values.

The Judge bought the Braves with Mathewson's agreement to serve as the team's president. Neither the Judge nor the former ace pitcher had high expectations. However, Mathewson immediately began to make the rounds as the highly-visible leader of the team. Mathewson dispatched a season pass to Calvin Coolidge. "Silent Cal" wrote back with a characteristically brief and dryly witty note: "It is seldom that I have the opportunity to enjoy the game," he replied (with likely emphasis on the word "enjoy"). He concluded in a wry manner, given the team's low standing in its league, that he hoped he might "some day see your team win."

Some day seemed very far away as Mathewson and the Judge began to make their way through the so-called "smokers" or after dinner speeches at Boston's men's clubs and sporting groups. They were cheered and patted on the back. Then, after the speeches, privately, the leaders of the community all said much the same thing to the Braves' new owners. It was recalled by the Judge in his memoirs: "If you have a winner or a contender for the pennant the fans will fill your park and be glad to have the opportunity of paying to get in. But if you have a loser you couldn't get them to enter your park if you gave them tax exempt silver passes."

During Mathewson's tenure the Braves were not to experience filled parks. Mathewson, realistic and honest to a fault, knew the effort of rebuilding the shattered team, once the "Miracle Braves," would be unlikely and time-consuming, either way. When a new player, "Jocko" Conlon, who had been the Harvard shortstop, approached Mathewson for advice in choosing between business and the Braves, Mathewson replied without hesitating.

"Although I am sacrificing the club's equity in your contract in telling you this," he told Conlon, "I believe it is in your best interest to accept the business opportunity."

Marooned from mainstream major league baseball, Mathewson and his partner declined to innovate with diversions after a band hired to play popular tunes failed to interest those in the bleachers.

"When a fan attends a ball game," the Judge concluded from this experiment, "the intensity of his interest is such that he does not want any outside diversion to interfere."

A well-intended offer by a New York showman for a comic acrobat to play first base or to draw a crowd with his antics as a coach was declined.

They looked to put real talent on the field in Braves uniforms. The Judge led an indefatigable but only partly successful campaign to buy and trade the Boston Braves up into contention. The Judge once wasted half a night in a Chicago hotel room with Branch Rickey, then general manager of the Cardinals' farm system. Meeting the reporters who had stood by from six to midnight in hopes of a scoop, the Judge greeted them with an announcement and a "photo opportunity." Displaying his headgear, he deadpanned, "We have put through a trade. I just traded a good $10 hat with Mr. Rickey for this old hat. You will notice," he said, turning the item deftly with big catcher's hands, "there is a cigarette hole burned right through the felt of the one I got from him."

Mathewson, managing his health quietly, did not stay up all night. Instead, he made evening speeches in series, then returned to Saranac Lake frequently. As the Judge noted, "He was particularly happy about going to Saint Petersburg. He loved to play checkers with the old-timers who are so familiar in the 'Sunshine City.' As I recall it he never lost a checker match to any of these experts, and some of them were wonderfully fine players." (Bob Fuchs saw Mathewson play at least eight checkers experts and beat them all — blindfolded!)

The Judge and Mathewson together increased Braves salaries from $80,000 for the whole team in 1922 to over $200,000 in 1923. The Judge noted that Mathewson had gone over the payroll figures, then said, "If we want a first division club, we've got to pay major league salaries."

The Judge and Mathewson had done more than doubling salaries but the Braves players remained unsatisfied. Shortly before Mathewson died in 1925, a delegation of players headed by Mickey O'Neil, who was a catcher with the team in the early twenties, met with the Judge.

The Judge, not averse to innovation, thought that a profit-sharing arrangement might prove mutually advantageous. He was willing to make every member of the Braves his partner, he told them, sharing in the profits of the club.

During discussion, the Judge fleshed out his idea.

"Every one of you players is entitled to an increase over last year's contract," he told the delegation. "The older players are to receive a raise of $1,000 to $2,000, the first-year men from the minor leagues a boost of 25 to 50 percent."

He also noted other numbers to the group.

"There are 40 players on the roster at present but on June 15 that will be reduced to 25 players," the Judge explained, considering a potential profit-sharing arrangement. "The club would pay each player the equivalent of last year's contract and, in addition, give each player one-twenty-fifth of team profits in lieu of an increase. The club will stand all losses. You would only share in the profits. You would not be responsible for the losses."

The season before, the Judge recalled, the Braves had made a profit of $56,000. Including revenue from concessions and rental of Braves Field for football games, there was likelihood of profit again. In the event of a pennant race or World Series share, more money would be divided.

O'Neil spoke up to clarify what sounded like an interesting proposition. "You mean, if the club showed a profit of $250,000, each one of the players would receive $10,000 in addition to his regular salary?"

The Judge affirmed, this was exactly so.

O'Neil asked permission to hold a meeting of all the players to discuss the matter. The Judge agreed.

O'Neil reported back the next day to the Judge.

"They prefer to take their regular increases," he said, "and let you worry about the profits."

Among others behind O'Neil was Johnny Cooney. Rhode Island Johnny Cooney had balked at signing with the Red Sox when he learned that they paid by check. In 1921 the Braves still paid their players in cash; Cooney joined the Tribe. He pitched for the team 1921 through 1930, his trademark being the balk or "hesitation pitch," depending on the umpire. Cooney's pitching days ended in 1930 when X-rays were taken of his arm. The doctors, told to figure out why he was weakening in late innings, found that his bones were already in 13 pieces — two main bones and eleven fragments.

His borderline pitch was not his only baseball skill, however; he moved on to other baseball work, leaving the Braves. On Casey Stengel's authority, his ability as an outfielder was on a par with Joe DiMaggio's. Cooney's nonpitching career with the Dodgers and Yankees shows he became more tolerant about accepting checks. He was with the Braves and White Sox as a coach in the forties and fifties. Cooney as pitcher-outfielder-coach also once served as home plate umpire until the official arrived to a game in progress. Can anyone match Johnny Cooney for that range of baseball versatility?

The team payroll expanded once by mistake, when the Judge and Mathewson claimed Giants pitcher Gearin for short money, a figure they had assumed would be the standard waiver price of the day, $4,000. What had happened before — and now happened to them — was that a hidden string (the term "purchase player," without a stated figure or any other description) on the waiver document catapulted a player onto the Braves roster at a far higher figure. The Judge and Mathewson resisted paying the $35,000 demanded by the Giants for this "purchase player" they had claimed on a waiver, and the matter was brought to Commissioner Kenesaw Mountain Landis for adjudication. Landis presided at a hearing at New York's Commodore Hotel to determine whether Gearin was the Braves' newest pitcher and, if so, for $4,000 as the Braves said or for $35,000 as the Giants demanded.

The Judge described the hearing, during which Landis made an initially unfavorable ruling, but then he nonetheless sustained the Braves' contentions.

Giants Secretary James Tierney was the first witness. He produced in evidence the waiver request which stated 'Purchase player.' He then introduced into evidence the agreement with the Milwaukee club, showing the purchase price to be $35,000. He also introduced the rules of the National League, which imposed the duty on the claiming party to ascertain the amount of the purchase price.

Judge Landis asked Secretary Tierney, "Did you receive from me a letter in which I ordered the clubs to put the amounts of the purchase price in the wavier request?"

Tierney answered, "I do not recall, but we are governed by the rules of our league in all these transactions."

Judge Landis said, "I know nothing about your rules, but I came to the conclusion several weeks ago that it was unfair to the claiming club not to be notified about the amount of the purchase price in the waiver request."

Turning to his secretary, Leslie O'Connor, Judge Landis asked to see his correspondence with the Giants.

Tierney then said, "Assuming that such a letter was received by the New York club, you made a definite ruling, Judge Landis, that where there is no meeting of the minds between two clubs affecting the purchase of a player, and the purchasing club uses such a player in an official game, such club loses all its rights and defenses."

Judge Landis turned to me and said, "Judge Fuchs, is that a fact, did you use the player in an official game?"

My answer was, "Yes."

Judge Landis said, "Mr. Tierney, did you give permission for that player to be used?"

Tierney answered, "No, under no circumstances."

Judge Landis then asked President Stoneham, "As president of the New York club, Mr. Stoneham, did you give permission pending negotiations for Boston to use pitcher Gearin?"

"Absolutely not," replied Stoneham. "I would not think of such a thing."

Judge Landis then said, "That being so, I am compelled to find the judgment of $35,000 in favor of the New York club against the Boston club."

"Just a minute," was heard from the back of the room, "before you make that decision, I want to be heard." It was John McGraw.

Judge Landis said, "Take the witness stand and make your statement, Mr. McGraw."

McGraw said, "I am the vice president of the New York club. Mr. Stoneham, president of the club, was in Philadelphia with the Giants, when Christy Mathewson and Judge Fuchs came to our New York office a week ago last Saturday.

"They were leaving for Brooklyn where the Braves were playing the Dodgers. I suggested to them to pitch Gearin and gave them my word

Judge Kenesaw Mountain Landis, Boston Braves president Christy Mathewson and Braves owner and vice president Judge Fuchs in 1923 (from the Robert S. Fuchs Collection).

that it would not prejudice their case or have any bearing on it. I was acting as the official head of the New York club that day, and I would rather pay the entire amount myself than to get a judgment on what might seem like deception on my part."

Judge Landis said, "That alters the situation entirely. The Commissioner is not bound by any technicalities but by the ordinary rules of justice, and I now decide that either the player be awarded to the Boston club for $4,000 or, if the New York club desires the player because of the understanding, the Boston club will return him without cost to either party."

Pitcher Gearin's one-game career with the Boston Braves was over, at no cost to the team after all, though it still stands in his official record in any baseball encyclopedia.

Another, later ruling by Judge Landis provided the partners with only temporary possession again; this time not of a pitcher but of $10,000. Bob Smith, a first baseman with a good throwing arm, was picked up from a Class A club for $10,000. When Judge Landis found fault with the Class A club (for having held onto Smith one season too many, hiding him illegally from a previous player draft while he developed) he fined the Class A club exactly the $10,000 it had received for their star. But who was to receive the fine? Judge Landis gave written instructions in a letter to Mathewson and the Judge, who were together in New York for a Giants-Braves game at the Polo Grounds. The partners asked Mr. and Mrs. Smith to breakfast with them at the hotel.

After what must have been a puzzling morning meal for the newly-married couple, the Judge told his player about the fine and handed him a check for $10,000.

Whatever Mr. Smith might otherwise have done with the money, in Mrs. Smith's presence he handed the check over, saying, "God bless Judge Landis!"

Check in hand, the happy couple promptly bought their Peachtree Street dream house in Atlanta that first season Bob Smith played with the Boston Braves.

Although teams at the bottom rarely rise, the Braves began their ascent in 1925. The Braves of 1925 were a hitting ball club. Evidence of a Braves' "lively ball" was evident on April 10, 1925, when Bernie Neis tapped a ball over the fence during batting practice, an event Ty Cobb had predicted would never happen, and which never had from the time Braves Field opened on August 18, 1915, to that date.

Christy Mathewson missed it. By 1925, "Big Six" was struggling with a body that was falling away from his control. On April 8, 1925, he wrote his partner from Saranac Lake his final note, a short one:

"I am not going to be able to leave here Friday for Boston but I do expect to feel well enough to arrive next Tuesday."

The season that had begun with that batting practice bounce ended with a bang. It was a wild ride and it still took a "September Sprint" but the team took fifth place in the National League that year. During the team's so-called "September Sprint" in 1925 the team flew up from last place to fifth place, a pace that proved impossible to keep up. The team had touched the edge of the first division of its National League. With luck there would be better to come in 1926. The first division was only the least of the possibilities. The Judge arranged to attend the World Series of 1925 with a great deal of pride.

That Series was fought between Pittsburgh and Washington.

When he wrote his memoirs of his years with Christy Mathewson, he described the end exactly as the news had come to him, during the World Series to which both of their energies had been bent and which had started to look difficult rather than impossible for their fledgling athletes. The Judge wrote:

> It was the night after the first game of the World Series of 1925 in Pittsburgh. The Senators with Walter Johnson pitching had beaten the Pirates

4 to 1 that afternoon. The baseball writers had finished their stories for the home town papers and the telegraph instruments in the wire room at the Hotel Schenley were clicking away the descriptions of the game and the color that surrounded it through space for the newspapers of the nation.

The baseball writers were relaxing upstairs in the Braves' quarters. There was a bridge game going on and another group was harmonizing the popular songs of the time. Every once in a while the card players would pause in their game and join in the harmony.

I can recall Nick Flatley of the *American*, Paul Shannon of the *Post*, Burt Whitman of the *Herald*, Austen Lake of the *Transcript*, Ed Cunningham of the *Traveler* and Uncle Jim O'Leary of the *Globe*.

Their day's work was done. There would be another game tomorrow, provided it did not rain, but tomorrow was another day. This was a night for relaxation and song.

As I recall it Uncle Jim O'Leary had been summoned from the room and someone was pinch hitting for him in the bridge game — holding cards in one hand — until he returned.

When the merriment was at its height, the door was suddenly opened and Uncle Jim stood at the entrance.

"Boys, just a minute, please. You couldn't have heard the news," Uncle Jim said. There was a momentary pause, then he continued, "Matty is dead."

One of the earliest sea planes was tried out by Judge Fuchs and baseball's first commissioner, Judge Kenesaw Mountain Landis, around 1925 in St. Petersburg, Florida, site of training camp for the Boston Braves and the New York Yankees (from the Robert S. Fuchs Collection).

The Judge reported the silence. Mathewson's death had been unexpected. Mathewson had never exposed the extent to which his condition had deteriorated, as he lost his ability to breathe finally altogether. The Judge recalled, when he had visited the Mathewsons at Saranac Lake three weeks before the Series, hearing Mathewson tell his wife, "Don't let's have any talking. I want to see the Judge immediately." He felt he knew now what their "talking" had been about; Jane confirmed it when he questioned her later, after Mathewson's death. Years before, in the hour between phone calls with the Judge at the Lambs Club, Mathewson's doctor told him that he would live three or four years away from Saranac but indefinitely if he stayed in seclusion.

She told him also about Mathewson's last request, how he had planned the details; on his death bed, he had instructed his wife, "I would like to have you engage a drawing room. I will be in the funeral car. When my body reaches the city of New York, I want to have the funeral procession pass the Polo Grounds on Eighth Avenue and then take my body down through the city to the Pennsylvania Station. I want to pass through the city of my affection, as it meant so much to me throughout my life."

The Judge, to whom New York also meant nearly everything, could only have empathized. Jane told the Judge that his last words, stated as he was calm and game facing death as he had been in facing life, were, "Jane, I am at peace with God and man. I have had a beautiful life. Don't grieve. We have had our share of God's blessings. Tomorrow I want you to take me to my last resting place overlooking Bucknell College. That's where I first met you." He repeated that he wanted his body to pass through New York and Lewisburg, Pennsylvania, concluding to her, "In those two places I enjoyed my greatest happiness and blessings."

On the day of his funeral the World Series game at Washington was interrupted. A crowd of 36,000 stood in silent prayer. Players of both teams bared their heads. Some wept. The American flag was lowered to half mast as a bugler sounded taps.

"Without Matty, I was compelled to undertake the presidency of the club and endeavored to do what I could to protect my investment, which meant that I practically gave up my law practice in New York and, for the next ten seasons, I was hopeful that we could establish a contending ball club," the Judge wrote, reconstructing this critical point of departure.

Christy Mathewson, whom the Judge and George M. Cohan had seen pitch three shutouts against Connie Mack's Athletics in the 1905 World Series, who had been the eyes of honest baseball at the 1919 World Series, was dead.

And Uncle Jim O'Leary had lost a partner, the one bridge player at the table who cared whether the old man held his cards with one hand or with two.

The finest tribute to Matty was written by the great sportswriter of the *New York Herald Tribune,* W.O. McGeoyan:

THE BAYARD OF BASEBALL

It was fitting that the distinctively American sport should produce the best beloved of all American athletes. This country with zest for sports is prone to make popular idols out of very common clay. But the national hero that baseball produced was worthy of all the affection and adulation that was felt for him by the youth and manhood of the land.

He was a Giant of the Giants and now that he is gone the athlete heroes before and since seem like pygmies.

He played the game to the last and not to the gallery. He never wrangled with the umpires. It was in that spirit that he lived and it was in that spirit that he died, clear eyed and courageous.

In the comparably inconsequential game of baseball he was truly great. There has never been his peer. But in the greater game of life he was greater.

6

Casey Stengel's First Manager's Job

> *"I must have splendid ownership."*
> — Casey Stengel, starting to list what he
> must have to succeed in baseball when he
> testified before the Kefauver Committee

When John McGraw announced that the Giants were trading Casey Stengel, Bill Cunningham and Dave "Beauty" Bancroft with the Braves for pitcher Joe Oeschger and outfielder Billy Southworth in 1924, he told reporters that he was not only doing it for the good of baseball but also "to do something big for my old friend, Matty."

McGraw sentimentally still kept a framed photo of his former ace on his desk at his Polo Fields office.

For his part the Judge homed in on wanting "a player-manager who was not only a player of ability but who was a quick thinker and added color to the club."

Did he find what he was looking for in the trio from New York?

He certainly did.

It was Dave "Beauty" Bancroft who the Judge felt was pick of the litter, whom he promoted to manager of the Braves when he arrived.

Casey Stengel remained a player, despite bad legs.

Bancroft, tough on punctuality at morning practice, precipitated bathroom fights as six players competed for rights to use one bathroom. It was said that he was "giving baseball a black eye." Neither Casey Stengel nor the other Braves rose to the heights envisioned for them by either their manager nor owner. The Judge mulled over what to do with Casey in particular. Observing that Casey was not burning up the baselines during the season of 1924, he spoke about an opportunity in the West — west of Boston, in Worcester. The Judge described it: "We were operating a team in Worcester at the time. I told Casey he could have the job as manager there if he desired. He accepted and took charge of the club."

In their negotiations, the Judge offered control to Stengel, telling him that he would not only be player-manager but president of the club.

Stengel had had a poor year playing in 1924. He was 33 years old. It was time. Stengel began as player-manager with the Braves' Class A Eastern League Worcester team in May 1925, and its president.

"He showed ability right from the start," the Judge recalled, "and did a good job with the team. Everything was going along smoothly until one day I picked up a newspaper and read that Casey had been appointed manager of the Toledo club of the American Association.

"Nothing had been said to me. He had not been given his release. We went through the correspondence of the Worcester club to see if any light could be thrown on the matter."

The Judge was given two letters to examine. The first read:

> Mr. Charles D. Stengel, President
> Worcester Ball Club
> Worcester, Massachusetts.
>
> Dear Mr. Stengel:
>
> Having an opportunity improve my position by going to a higher classification as manager, I hereby tender my resignation as manager of the Worcester club. I cannot leave without thanking you for your courtesy, consideration and advice, which was of great help in running the club.
>
> Very truly yours,
> Casey Stengel

The second, in reply, read:

> Mr. Casey Stengel
> Worcester Ball Club
> Worcester, Massachusetts
>
> Dear Casey:
>
> Your letter came as a surprise but we realize that ability should be rewarded. Therefore, I join with the fans of Worcester in expressing our appreciation for your outstanding services rendered and wish you luck in your new position. We congratulate Toledo on getting your valuable services.
>
> Very truly yours,
> Charles D. Stengel

When Commissioner Landis asked the Judge if he should take action to stop the transfer, the Judge answered without hesitation. "My reply was twofold," the Judge explained. "I still retained a sense of humor and, of course, I had no desire to stop Casey's progress and would have granted him his release if he had requested it."

Stengel, who became wealthy later through business and banking investments, was suckered into the move to Toledo. As he later complained at the Judge's 80th birthday dinner, "I found Toledo in trouble. I immediately had to invest $8,000 of my own money to keep the team from folding up!" (He did not confide to the crowd whether he got a return on that investment.)

The Judge's friendship with Stengel was lifelong and continued to stimulate his sense of humor. When, during the fifties, he and Stengel sat together on the train from Boston to New York, the Judge mentioned that Branch Rickey had written a book in which Rickey referred to Stengel as "the one clown who could play Hamlet."

Casey looked at the Judge and had two questions.

"Is that good?" was the first.

"Where can I buy the book?" was the second.

The Judge took the same train trip as an opportunity to seek Stengel's recollection of an event during his Pittsburgh year, 1918.

> There was one out in the ninth inning and the Pirates were one run behind. Casey was on third base and a fly-ball was hit to the outfield. Casey tagged up and ran to the plate. The throw from the outfield was high but the catcher managed to touch Casey with the ball before Casey touched the plate.
>
> After the game, Mr. Dreyfus sent for Casey and asked him, "Is there any doubt in your mind that if you had slid into the plate, you would have been safe and tied the game?"
>
> Casey's answer was, "Sure, but for the kind of money you are paying, I don't slide."

The Judge had discovered — and lost — a talented manager. He had lost his team partner, the gutsy Christy Mathewson. He started to champion good sportsmanship himself.

His first season without Christy Mathewson, 1926, provides a good example of the Judge's application of "fair ball." Paul Shannon of the Boston *Post* had dinner with the Judge and two Braves pitchers, Larry Benton and Bob Smith (the Smith with the house in Atlanta). Benton and Smith were to face the Cardinal batters. As Shannon was told and later reported, both favored the Cards over their archrivals of the time, the Cincinnati Reds. It was already September and it looked like it would come down to these two for the pennant. Sympathy aside, Benton beat the Cards first, then Smith won the next day.

With no pennant at stake, the team played the best possible ball. Their record in September 1926 includes taking three out of four games from the Cardinals, four out of five from the Cubs and all three from the Reds.

Ironically, although the Braves killed the Cards' chances with pitchers' regrets, the three-game sweep also killed the Reds' chance for the 1926 pennant. Spoilers, beating league leaders, almost First Division, honest contenders, his Braves pleased the Judge. The *Globe* at the time reported the scores and told the story: "The Braves looked more like champions than any of the champions." The Tribe was beating teams convincingly at last, with only one consistent .300 batter but a terrific defensive network. They needed a batsman. They found one in Rogers Hornsby.

7

Rogers Hornsby at the Plate

"Did you hear? The Judge traded Rogers Hornsby for $200,000 and five machine-guns from Chicago."
— Will Rogers (1928)

"I don't smoke, drink or chew. I can hit to the left, center and right. They call me a great player. If you do like I do, you can be a great player, too."
— Rogers Hornsby to the Braves upon assuming the managerial slot (1928).

Rogers Hornsby was a steak eater. Whether his taste developed in his early years back in Texas or after he had considered and decided what should be the diet of an athlete, Hornsby loved steak with a passion. He ate steak every night. He refused dinner invitations unless steak was on the menu. People came to know to ask him to a steak dinner, with emphasis on the "steak." Friendship with him could be built on steak. Although Hornsby was a somewhat aloof manager he somehow learned that Bunny Hearn, the Braves' new pitcher from the New York–Pennsylvania League, a diminutive lefthander, liked steak but could not afford it. Hornsby used to take Hearn to the best steakhouses on the road — he knew them all — and, while enjoying a steak himself, enjoyed Hearn's enjoyment.

If Hornsby ate steak to live, though, he lived for baseball. If he had to give up steak for baseball, he probably would have. He actually did forego movies for the game. At a time when movies were the most popular and the cheapest form of mass entertainment, when movie theaters broke records unequaled ever since, there was no seat for Hornsby. By his own superstitious belief that the flickering light of the movies might adversely affect his eyes, he boycotted movies altogether. As manager in 1928 he told the Braves not to attend movies. He explained why; only his buddy dared take issue.

"The movies don't flicker any more," Hearn informed his chief. Hopefully his remark did not interrupt their dinner engagements.

Hornsby was one of the rare ballplayers (not to be confused with baseball fans or baseball reporters) who, apart from eating steak, dedicated most of his waking hours to baseball. He played baseball or talked baseball. The only other entertainment, flickering or not, which he indulged was horse racing; otherwise, for Hornsby, it was baseball, baseball, baseball!

His concentration caused records to cluster about him. Up until 1947 Hornsby was the only player to win two Triple Crowns. (Ted Williams captured his second in 1947.)

Hornsby, outspoken in the extreme, arrived on the Braves and left the Braves by virtue of his habit of speaking frankly. His candor, unappreciated by John McGraw, was appreciated by the Judge. Hornsby thought out loud. One knew where the "Rajah" stood. He held nothing back and, given concentration exclusively on baseball, he occasionally let slip opinions and judgments of his owners and managers that others would have left unsaid.

Partners John McGraw and Charlie Stoneham, down a few pegs from their heyday seasons and more sensitive than ever about the opinions of others concerning their professional skills in running their team, had not heard the "Rajah" speak ill of them but their loyal secretary, Jim Tierney, had.

Tierney, who had been riding in a crowded elevator at the Shanley Hotel in Pittsburgh, his presence not noticed by players including Hornsby, heard an unguarded candid quip that he passed onto his employers. (Presumably, reference to Rajah's superior managing when McGraw had been absent in 1927 — that it "paid off" for McGraw to be away.)

The repetition of such a casual comment from the loud and outspoken player doomed his Giants career. It was the proverbial straw that broke the employer's back when the employee is enjoying a better year than the employer. McGraw and Stoneham advanced in priority a plan considered for a while, to relieve themselves of a critic who spoke out as thoughts struck him. After all, Hornsby was a man not only of immense physical stature but held in awe by others, most of whom knew of him from newspapers and newsreels before seeing him in the flesh and taking part in the sport alongside him. Hornsby acted the part of leader and stood somewhat aloof from others as his virtual right. There was no room in the Polo Grounds for two managers, one official and the other unofficial and both at odds with one another.

But where could the Giants place their terror?

It might be cynical to imagine but hardly inappropriate to say that the Boston Braves came to mind. The Braves would be "punishment duty" for Hornsby. While the Boston team even so would do no great harm to the Giants.

The Judge was asked to come up from Pinehurst, North Carolina, where he had been vacationing, to meet McGraw and Stoneham. This particular summons to New York was a pleasure to accept.

His meeting with McGraw was historic. When the New York chapter of the Baseball Writers' Association of America met next, the question and answer from the rostrum was:

"Who's the biggest thinker in baseball today?"

"Judge Fuchs is the biggest thinker in the world — he thinks Shanty Hogan and Jimmy Welsh are worth $250,000."

For that was the deal — Rogers Hornsby, highest-salaried player of the National League, often compared with Babe Ruth, for a player just beyond his rookie year and a catcher brought up from the minor leagues. Sports writers told to expect an important announcement from the Giants' front office put money on their guesses. Many expected Hornsby's promotion to succeed McGraw as manager. None imagined the team would trade away its leading player.

(Ironically, the deal got better — he even got Hogan back for the Braves, for $10,000 in 1932.) Recognizing that Hogan had home-run potential provided there were "windows" in the fences of Braves Field, the Judge literally redesigned the park for his player, intending Hogan to be a star. However, his hitting home runs became rare, despite the so-called "jury box" extension of bleachers out onto left field, moving it 50 feet closer to home plate, 402 to 353 feet, centerfield fence 150 feet closer, 550 to 387 feet. Hogan, who had scored 48 runs with the Giants in 1928 and 60 in 1930, while his home runs soared from 3 to 13 a season, did not bat consistently back in Boston. Opposing team batters did. They hit two over the fence for every one of the Braves' homers. Hogan's problem was his weight. He never stopped eating and, unlike Hornsby, did not require steak.

"We tried to save Shanty from himself," Bob Fuchs recalls. When he was president of the Braves' Harrisburg farm-team, they had a catcher, Ray Mueller, later a major leaguer but in 1934 not quite ready.

"They called us a farm team but almost never called any player up to Boston, until one day we got the call for Ray. What happened was Shanty

Hall of Famers Rogers Hornsby and Ty Cobb (courtesy of the Boston Public Library, Print Department).

was eating himself out of baseball. Everything they did to force him to control his weight was unsuccessful. So they decided to give him a scare by calling up one of the farm team boys to his position. When it worked, or started to work — nothing worked long to separate Shanty from his food — Ray was sent back down to Harrisburg. He later became a good player in his own right, but he owed his major league debut to Shanty Hogan's eating habits."

(Hogan did eat himself out of the game, by 1937.)

The presence of Rogers Hornsby on the Braves roster was not an unmixed blessing but presented an immediate problem for the Judge and his new partner, Charles Francis Adams. The Judge had found a partner and kindred spirit in Adams, an enthusiastic sportsman with money who had a keen appreciation of athletic talent and was willing to pay to get it. Six feet tall and wiry as a track star himself, Adams's motto was "pay cash" and "owe nothing to anybody." The owner of a chain of supermarkets throughout New England, he had purchased the Boston Bruins cheaply and in the thirties was to build a race track, Suffolk Downs, to bring thoroughbred racing to Boston for the first time. The Boston Braves had a future, he was sure.

An intermediary, Wesley Preston, who published the *Boston Herald*, got the Judge together with Adams at the Exchange Club in downtown Boston. Just as the lunch at the Lambs Club had quickly produced a change in ownership, so did this lunch. The Judge explained that one of his partners wanted to sell out for a quarter-million. Adams asked the Judge to go with him to his office nearby, at 41 Milk Street. Once there, Adams handed the Judge $250,000 in cash and sought no receipt or contract.

"Buy him out," Adams told the Judge, waving away any suggestion that there be a written document of the transaction. He said, "If I didn't have confidence in you, I wouldn't join with you."

The Judge, thrilled to be sought as a partner by a man whose word was his bond, took the money without signing anything. He promptly went over to the Exchange Bank, which held a promissory note and mortgage on the partner's Braves stock, paid off the note with interest, and placed the profit on account for the investor.

The Judge returned to state the news. Adams was out. Thinking Adams as a businessman had probably written up some type of document for signature, much as he had waved off its necessity earlier, he asked the secretary. "Did Mr. Adams leave a note or agreement for me to sign for the money he gave me?"

"Yes," was the answer, and the agreement was found and placed before the Judge who, in a flamboyant reciprocal act, signed it conspicuously before the woman without reading it.

The Judge and Adams had hired a new manager, South Boston's Jack Slattery.

Slattery was by far the most popular man ever to serve as Braves manager. A native son who had started with the Red Sox in 1903 (like Casey Stengel, he had graduated from dental school but never became a dentist), an injury fated him to coach. He had been baseball coach at Tufts and Harvard — where he had taken Fred Mitchell's place when Mitchell had become Braves manager — and, finally, at Boston College. To be an Irish Catholic South Boston former Red Sox player and Boston College baseball coach was to be highly recommended in Boston in 1927.

When the Judge and Adams talked about Slattery, they spoke of Slattery's following:

"Mr. Adams said to me, 'I know how we can fill Braves Field, new seats, and all,'" the Judge told a banquet group. "Naturally I was interested and asked how. 'Give a pass to each of Jack Slattery's friends,' he said, 'and the Field will not hold them all.'"

The dilemma which had existed on the Polo Grounds between John McGraw and Rogers Hornsby had been a fairly even match. But Braves Field, though larger, was also too small for two managers, especially if the unofficial manager knew more about baseball. The partners smelled trouble coming and when Slattery called for no meeting at spring training in St. Petersburg, the partners called for one with him. When they asked about what they already knew, Slattery admitted to difficulties. He was manager but everybody who came in asked, "Where's Hornsby?" or "Which one is Hornsby?" and so forth, causing distraction and reducing his sense of control or status to nothing.

The Judge picked up on the question and quipped, as if in reply to the question of which one is Hornsby, "Turn around and watch for the player who has three bats in his hand and that is Hornsby."

Slattery, who had originally described himself as "elated" to have had the "great luck to have such a player as Hornsby handed to me in my first year as manager of a big league club," became less and less elated until he resigned after six weeks to permit active management of the team by Rogers Hornsby. Hornsby, "manager-player," excelled in both ways with the team, but the team itself was not up to any consistently high level of play. Hornsby achieved two major league records that year. As player, he was the only Boston Brave to lead the National League in season batting average in the twentieth century. He hit .387. As manager, at the very end of the 1928 season, he led the Braves through nine straight doubleheaders. No other team ever played more doubleheaders than the Braves under Hornsby did, during which streak the team set another record, losing five consecutive doubleheaders in September 1928.

At the end of 1928, having served his time in what he probably himself

Rogers Hornsby, the only Boston Brave of the modern era to lead the National League in hitting. He hit .387 in 1928, his only year with the club (courtesy of the Boston Public Library, Print Department).

understood to be "punishment duty," Hornsby judged that his owner would be open to a candid comment or two, and he judged the Judge rightly. He considered and said expressly that he and the Judge were not merely associates but good friends. Leaning on that relationship — Hornsby, like the Judge, lived at the Copley Plaza, where he had his steak and ate it, too, with good appetite, often joining the Judge at the hotel dining room to talk baseball and dine, business and pleasure at the same time and place — the great hitter sought to work out his own future.

"If you give me permission," he told the Braves owner, "I think I can talk to Mr. Wrigley, Senior, and trade myself to Chicago for a number of good, young players that will mean more to you than my individual services, which might only have another year to run."

The Judge, surprised by the idea but not displeased with Hornsby's candor, acknowledged his manager's sincerity and told him to see what he could do, giving him 30 days. After all, given the team's standing, the Braves were in no position to continue to pay Hornsby's $42,500 salary, the National League's largest, let alone increase it.

Within a week the Judge got a call from Bill Veeck, Sr., then president of the Cubs. A meeting was set up. The agenda was secret from anyone but those taking part: Wrigley and Veeck, and Cubs manager Joe McCarthy, meeting with the Judge and Adams.

A mid-way site was proposed — Buffalo, New York, where Adams was attending a national grocers' convention.

The Buffalo meeting was successful, but it went fast as a poker game played by good players.

First, Veeck announced what he thought would be a surprise: "Hornsby wants to come to Chicago. We'll be glad to have him. We'll give you a replacement on second base, Fred McGuire, plus $50,000."

Nobody said anything. Then the Judge (forewarned by Hornsby to make demands helpful to the Braves) declined.

"I'm looking for enough players from Los Angeles and Chicago to build up a ball club," he explained. "We are going to have Sunday baseball in Boston."

The serious, sincere delivery of the Judge's refusal, coupled with the shorthand for imminent prosperity and a turn-around for the Braves, encouraged the Cubs to huddle over another thought.

Adams interrupted the huddle. "I'll tell you," he said. "You are offering $50,000 for the champion batter of the National League. Let's face the situation, Mr. Veeck. We're here in the Statler Hotel, which has a bank in it. That bank will certify my check and I will give you a check for $250,000 for two of your ball players."

McCarthy, no doubt irritated by what he thought was a bluff, said: "Take him up on it," to his employers.

Adams ostentatiously took out a checkbook and began writing out the check.

Veeck, who had neither accepted nor declined, said, "Before I accept this check, of course, I've got to know which two players you want."

Adams specified immediately: Cuyler and Hartnett.

Adams handed over the check. "Get this certified at the hotel bank and draw up the purchase papers for Kiki Cuyler and Leo Hartnett right now."

Veeck held the check in his hands for a few moments, smiling cryptically. Then he shook his head.

"Mr. Adams, you certainly are a good business man. You know right well that Mr. Wrigley wouldn't take a million for those two. So what's your price for Hornsby?"

It came down to Hornsby for $200,000 and five players: Fred McGuire, two pitchers and two others. The Judge gunned for one more side-deal on Wally Berger, then playing for Los Angeles but under contract to the Cubs. He secured Berger for $40,000. (The Cubs later offered $250,000 for Berger, trying unsuccessfully to get him back in 1932.) The scale of the trade is best understood by comparing it to an earlier benchmark: 1920, when Harry Frazee sold Babe Ruth for $137,000 to the Yankees marked the previous high.

The Buffalo deal, behind which Hornsby stood an invisible presence but moving force, secured for the Braves their best years of competitiveness. With Adams, the Judge had made the best deal of his life. But for Joe McCarthy — so quick to suggest acceptance of a money deal for two players unnamed — the trade meant a rival, and Hornsby did, indeed, replace him as manager within a month of his arrival. He had the last word, telling the Judge accurately, "When this thing is all over, you know what's going to happen. Mr. Wrigley has his mind made up for Hornsby. He'll succeed me as manager."

And so it was.

The next season, the Cubs under Hornsby, won the pennant. And, with six new players from the Buffalo deal, the revitalized Braves started to slip into gear, climbing up the ladder toward a pennant themselves, both teams linked on the way up to the best right-handed batter in the game, the outspoken steak-eating non-movie-watching Rogers "Rajah" Hornsby.

Hornsby's release was a practical problem in public relations. Hornsby, hyped as a great star on the roster throughout 1928, would be leaving Boston after a year in a deal involving some $200,000. In Boston, which witnessed Babe Ruth's sale by Harry Frazee in 1920 for $105,000 and a $75,000 loan to put on a Broadway show, there was still a sour taste about such deals. The Judge managed to keep curses at bay. He gave Boston papers copies of Hornsby's affectionate letter of farewell, which many printed in full. Simultaneously, the many new players were attractively described. Because Hornsby could hardly be expected to stay — his appearance in Boston having been a virtual miracle — and it made baseball and business sense that the champion would go on to a better team, the Judge was not painted by the Frazee brush. Fans were rightly convinced that the Judge had put a lot of money into the "Sunday baseball" referendum campaign and the Hornsby deal, if it provided a dividend, has been earned. Indeed, the Braves would have been deep in red ink at the end of 1928 without the Hornsby deal. With it, the team's season loss was still $6,000.

8

The Sunday Baseball Flap

"I would feel a great deal better if you would stop making speeches."
— Judge Fuchs to John C. L.
Dowling, Chairman, Boston
Commission (January 2, 1929)

Just before Thanksgiving 1928, Judge Fuchs asked his new partner, Charles F. Adams, to stop by the Copley Plaza to hear that "some men had come in for a hold-up," people he called "Jesse James boys without horses."

The Judge, in an amused vein, described to Adams a proposal he had not taken seriously. He had been visited at his hotel suite by a barrelmaker turned boxing promoter, city councilors who had spun a yarn claiming that a dozen city councilors would hold up Sunday ball in Boston until each was paid $5,000.

Adams, less amused, spoke to others and a far less lighthearted rumor made its way to the ears of the Finance Commission, Boston's "watchdog," set in place by the Republican legislature to keep tabs on a Democratic city. The Fincom, as it was known, was a familiar front page, banner headline speechifying forum, to which the Brahmins had beat a retreat as the Irish took over city hall otherwise. Ever attuned to rumors and more than willing to conduct its investigations in public, the Fincom clearly wanted the Judge to put the finger on half the city council as corrupt extortionists unfit to hold any public office.

In late December 1928, the Fincom summoned the Judge and Adams to meet with it in executive session. When neither the Judge nor Adams would answer questions, the Fincom took predictably publicized actions.

Dowling secured a Supreme Judicial Court order from Associate Justice

Edward Pierce requiring the Judge, Adams and Braves' secretary Ed Cunningham to testify to what each knew of a plot. Of course, neither Adams nor Cunningham had first-hand knowledge and the Judge's knowledge was limited to what he had been told during an exchange the Judge had failed to take seriously. The Judge was, therefore, the only man in the spotlight and the first and main witness.

To accommodate crowds numbering in the thousands, the Fincom hearing was held at the Gardiner Auditorium of the State House. Elevator men got into the mood of things by taking people to the "ball game" while state troopers directed people to "Braves Field" and patrolled the aisles of the "bleachers." Photographers flashed pictures and cartoonists scrambled to caricature the participants. Seats in the first two rows were reserved for the city councilors named as constituting the conspiracy to hold up Sunday baseball.

City councilors responded with variously-phrased denials of wrongdoing.

As reported in the Boston *Globe*, Councilor John F. Dowd denounced the Judge's ultimate testimony as "95 percent lies." He added that the Judge was greedy and that "love of money drove the Boston College team, a Catholic group, from Braves Field because of the fact that they would not allow the Judge most of the gate receipts."

"There is a nigger in the woodpile somewhere," Councilor Motley said with equally bald bigotry. "To me Billy Lynch is the kindest, whitest and greatest little fellow I know." (Billy Lynch was the alleged ringleader.)

Although first terming the Judge's testimony "a pretty good bedtime story," Motley later grumbled that "it appears someone talked out of turn, and the Judge has also talked too much."

Councilor Thomas McMahon (who had voted to table the Sunday baseball approval measure in December), cautiously distanced himself from the others and hedged his denial: "If there are any dishonest fellows in the council, they are bringing honest men into it just because they voted to table, too."

Councilor Robert G. Wilson ducked deftly behind baseball lingo. "They are coming too fast for me," he told a reporter. "It's all over my head." Another maligned the Judge's motives, forgetting that Fuchs had not wanted to testify. By this theory, the Judge, a close friend of the president of the Boston city council, was supposed to "knock off Billy Lynch as a presidential possibility."

But overall the accused councilors huddled close to their ethnic base. Blarney thickened the air. Councilor Murphy's substantiation of his character, that he had a conscience and believed in fair play, was rooted in his being "an Irishman, one of those who for 700 years endured persecution."

For the Judge the stakes could not have been higher. His very ownership of the Braves was on the line: Just as when Benny Kauff was acquitted, a transcript of the answers given would be scrutinized by Commissioner Landis. It became the Judge's job to put together a record not only for the Boston public but for Commissioner Landis. He accomplished both tasks with great success.

The experienced trial lawyer in him knew what he was doing, and knew that it was contrary to what the Fincom was doing. The Fincom wanted to publicize the possibility of corruption. The Judge merely wanted to tell his story and defend his honor. When Chairman Dowling got in the way, the Judge invited attention to it.

"I would feel a great deal better if you would stop making speeches," he told Dowling in a challenge that aroused such a clamor among the Braves fans in attendance that Dowling was led to a gavel-pounding threat to stop the hearing altogether.

The hearing, originally and always supposedly concerned with reconstructing a midnight chat at the Judge's hotel suite, metamorphosed into a character study of the Judge's entire professional life, including his New York years.

Ludicrously, one of the councilors insisted that he would bring forward "proof" that the Judge's service on the bench had been only to take a vacationing judge's place for 30 days. The Judge, of course, had served three years and his resignation was accepted with a letter of regret by Chief Justice McAdoo. A colorful jurist in a colorful court during a colorful period of New York history, the Judge's doings had made news. Once even *The New York Times* had run a small article about his reduction of fines on the basis of the war-time increased cost of living. Needless to say, the councilor delivered no such "proof."

More ominously, Boston newspapers recycled old news. The Judge had represented Arnold Rothstein (accused of "fixing" the 1919 World Series). The Judge had, indeed, successfully defended Rothstein from an indictment for murder of two police officers killed during a gambling raid. When a Boston reporter checking the decade-old court file discovered some of the papers were missing, the discovery ran in Boston as news.

People in Boston were encouraged to wonder about the Judge and most of those people were Irish Catholics. Seizing the right card to play at the right moment, the Judge sought a quick, short endorsement from Al Smith.

Al Smith, not well remembered today, was more prominent and more popular in Boston in the twenties than the man who beat him for president, Herbert Hoover. Smith, a Catholic, had been voted for by two of Boston's voters in November 1928, to every one for Hoover. His popularity endured past his defeat, which was blamed on bigotry. In the 1932 primary Smith handily defeated Franklin D. Roosevelt as the Boston Democrats' favorite son. And, as the Fincom hearings took place in January, 1929, the endorsement of Judge Fuchs by Al Smith meant something.

Smith's telegraph back to the Judge: "I have known Emil E. Fuchs for more than 25 years during all of which time he has been a respectable citizen of New York and much esteemed by bench and bar as well as by leading citizens of both political parties." This provided the Judge with rebuttal to slurs on his character, supposed by New York scandals and the taint of partisanship. A man good in Al Smith's book was, to the Boston Catholic, good in anybody's book.

A similar endorsement came in from Father Duffy of New York's famed "Fighting Sixty-Ninth," from Monsignior Corry and prominent members of the bench and bar as well as leading men of business and baseball (see Appendix A).

Although Catholic icons had given their respective imprimaturs to the Judge's charges against Irish Catholics, the Judge himself had not initiated the investigation, nor did he seek prosecution of any councilor. Indeed, as he testified at the hearings, he could not take a "hold up" threat very seriously. Sunday baseball was too popular to be stopped. The referendum showed that. The history in other states showed it. In Boston, to oppose Sunday baseball was political poison, if not suicide.

During the hearings it came out that Charles F. Adams had targeted an anti–Sunday baseball legislator, Senator Bilodeau of Dorchester, for extinction. The Judge followed up by permitting the Braves game announcer, "Stonewall" Jackson, to run against Bilodeau in the primary. Jackson's presence was not to beat Bilodeau but to highlight Bilodeau's opposition to Sunday baseball and, thus, turn the voters to the challenger. Jackson as candidate distributed 5,000 expired Braves game tickets stamped on the reverse side with his picture and "Vote for Jackson." The Braves rightly expected to keep their announcer out of the senate (he got a few hundred votes) and hoped to weaken Bilodeau's political base enough that the incumbent fell from power. He did, losing the primary and his chance for reelection narrowly. Bilodeau and his cohorts never forgot or forgave the ploy.

Ironically, "Stonewall" Jackson's Braves tickets were violations of the

Massachusetts corporate statutes, which forbade a corporation from giving anything of value to defeat a candidate standing for public office in an election. The Suffolk County District Attorney became the unwitting avenger of Bilodeau's loss when he brought criminal charges against the Judge for violation of Massachusetts law. The Dorchester Democrat's last hurrah led Judge Fuchs to face the wrong side of the bench for the first and only time in his life. By pleading *nolo contendere*, paying a fine and resolving the criminal case without a record of conviction, he could potentially avert catastrophe before Commissioner Landis and certainly stymie any civil suit by Bilodeau, which might have been brought had the Judge stood trial and been convicted. The Judge, thus, pled *nolo*.

As to the city council bloc, real or imaginary, it came to nothing. Sunday baseball — of which Major Lynch declared himself ever an "unwavering" supporter who had voted to table the measure in December only "to look the bill over, to study its contents" — was approved.

9

Here Comes the Judge!

"Fuchs has been losing ball games and money hand over fist, handing huge sums to managers. Naturally, it occurred to him that these birds didn't know any more than he did."
— Nick Flatley

"I promised Chief Justice McAdoo when I resigned from the bench that I would return some day and I have."
— Judge Fuchs, on taking over as Braves manager (1929)

Up to and a season after Christy Mathewson's death the Braves had been on an upward trail: the 44-game spread between the team and first place in 1923, exactly 40 in 1924, reduced to 25 in 1925 and shrank to 22 in 1926, a 50 percent improvement by this measure. In 1927 things fell apart and "Banny" Bancroft went, to be replaced by Rogers Hornsby — but that season, 1928, was worse.

In 1929 the Judge, at the suggestion of his new financial partner Charles Francis Adams, decided to manage the team himself.

For him to take over as owner-manager was for him to assume the achievement of John McGraw. McGraw, amused from a distance, sent the Judge a pair of trousers reinforced in a leather seat as a buffer against "squirming on the bench."

The Braves played and won a doubleheader set of exhibition games against the Athletics under unusual circumstances in 1929. Ty Cobb made it happen.

Connie Mack, a friend of the Judge's for years and wanting to do a favor for the Braves' new manager (the Judge), called about playing. He told the Judge that the Braves and Athletics had never played any spring training exhibition games against the other and that ought to be rectified. The Judge and Mack agreed upon games to be played at St. Petersburg, where the Braves trained, and Fort Meyers, the Athletics' spring camp. The home team was to keep the receipts.

"It was just like him to make that suggestion," the Judge wrote later of Mack. "He knew the Boston club would receive the better of it because St. Petersburg was much the larger city."

On game day when Ty Cobb was on deck, Eddie Collins at bat, and Frank Wilson was the home plate umpire, Cobb yelled a remark to Collins concerning Wilson's capacity. (Wilson and Cobb had long feuded with one another in the days both were in the American League.)

"One more remark like that and you're out of the game," the umpire said, Cobb not yet having even swung his bat.

Cobb challenged him: "Try and put me out!"

Wilson pulled out his watch.

"Unless you're off this field in one minute, I will forfeit the game to the Boston Braves."

It was a long minute in passing, Cobb and Wilson staring at one another as gunslingers of the Old West. Cobb did not move. Wilson did. He turned to stands, announced that the game was forfeited to the Braves and walked off the field, pulling the other umpires with him.

Mack hotfooted over to the Braves' dugout and raised with the Judge the option of keeping the crowd happy. Some 5,000 present would all want their money back for a game called in the first inning, he said, unless the Judge and he acted. He selected a fill-in umpire for the Athletics, Mickey Cochrane; the Judge selected Arthur Devlin, Braves coach, as their umpire. As they finalized matters to begin anew, Wilson reappeared on the playing field.

"The first game has been forfeited to the Boston Braves," Wilson said. "We will now play an exhibition game."

The crowd roared its approval.

Without a word, Cobb remained a player in the "second" game while Wilson served with Cochrane and Devlin umpiring that game.

The Braves took that exhibition game legitimately.

Incredibly, for a few weeks early in the 1929 season the Judge made a run for it. As to the pair of leather trousers reinforced at the seat from John McGraw, one sports writer said that the Judge "should send them back as Mack has done more squirming on the bench" (as of early May 1929). The Braves under the Judge racked up 7 wins and only 2 losses in their first nine games and, at .778, stood at the top of the National League's standings.

Cynics quickly urged the Judge to quit while he was ahead, with the glory of having taken his team to the top. Nobody (except the Judge?) thought it would last. And it did not last. At season's end, his tally was a slightly better team record than Hornsby had led the team to in 1928. Without any batsmen the likes of Hornsby, the Judge's performance falls right in the middle with three years when the team was better (1925, 1926, 1927) and three years it was worse (1923, 1924, 1928) than 1929. But the excitement came at the beginning when the team responded and pulled itself from last to first place. The Judge, eager to quit when he was ahead, offered the manager's job to Walter James Vincent "Rabbit" Maranville. He could not reach agreement with Rabbit Maranville to take the reins of what was offered him, at the moment the number one team in the league, because Maranville demanded a five-year contract. Maranville, who had seen the team in its best year and had been himself one of the heroes of the "Miracle Braves" that had gone to the World Series (four-game sweep) capping a meteoric rise from bottom- to top-rung league standing in 1914, was interested in managing.

But the well had been poisoned.

A confidential remark to a reporter led to an unauthorized story that the Judge was considering Maranville to take over as manager. The Judge recalled it as the only time a reporter violated the rules and published something given confidentially. With that publication not only giving Maranville a sense of bargaining leverage as a sought-after prize and time to seek out advice from others, he came to the table with a demand for a multiyear contract, a commitment that the Judge could not make to an untried manager.

Ed Cunningham, the Boston sports writer, said that Rabbit Maranville was "a boy who never grew up." Rules and records were made to be broken. Maranville hit the most career triples for the Boston Braves, had more career hits than any other player born in Massachusetts, and recorded for base more putouts (5,139) than any other shortstop. Maranville led the National League season after season in fielding percentage and double plays (5 times), putouts (7 times), and assists (4 times). He batted .308 in the World Series twice — in 1914 for the Braves, and in 1928 for the Cardinals. The first game of 1914 he went 3 for 4 against Christy Mathewson. He was a great player, easily voted into the Hall of Fame. But his place in baseball's lighter side is even more assured. For colorful antics, Maranville is up with Casey Stengel and Babe Ruth. On the field as well as off the field, Maranville enjoyed clowning. His so-called "vest pocket" catches charmed children and adults. He would taunt umpires, pulling a pair of eyeglasses out of his pocket and offering them, without a word. His elevation to managing did not change

Braves Manager Judge Fuchs (standing) with his "brain trust" (left to right) Rabbit Maranville, Hank Gowdy, George Sisler and Johnny Evers, circa 1929 (reprinted with permission of the *Boston Herald*).

him at all. He poured ice water over his sleeping comrades when he managed the Cubs in 1925. Locked into his room as a rowdy drunk one night while others played cards in the next room, he walked out onto the narrow ledge and, tapping on the window of the twelfth floor, waved at the gang from outside. Only five feet five inches, he was named "Rabbit" for his speed. He was fast, even into his forties. Bob Fuchs, who attended Rollins College in Florida, recalls a 1933 exhibition game for his alma mater at which players including Maranville took on the Rollins College girls' softball team. Maranville hit a single but kept running to second, third, and home safely. He then began to round the bases again; he made it three more times before the girls were able to tag him out!

In 1929 owner-manager Judge Fuchs needed Maranville and Maranville needed a spot. He had sworn off drinking (declaring that, as a result, after 1927 American alcohol consumption went way down) but still was benched by the Pirates. Maranville, at bat 672 times in 1922, the most in the National League, was only called upon 200 to 300 times a season. The Judge changed that. In Boston, he was at bat more than 500 times a season from 1929 to 1932. Although he struggled, he slipped from .284 to .281 to .260 to .235 to .218 as he went. But Maranville had "stuff"; Austen Lake recalled Maranville at bat in the last of the ninth inning one Sunday game. (On Sundays in the twenties there was a six o'clock curfew, by which the game ended and the game's score reverted to the score of the last completed inning.) Maranville hit 18 foul balls, stopping only when the curfew bell rang. Three runs from the first half of the ninth inning were deducted from the Cubs' tally and the Braves won!

Beginning in 1932 he switched from his legendary shortstop position to second base. Plainly, the old warhorse was winding down. But at spring training in 1934 when a rookie catcher blocked home plate as he was sliding, the Rabbit broke his leg in two places and was out the entire season. Will Rogers commented on the injury in his newspaper column: "When Rabbit

Rabbit Maranville and Nick Altrock (courtesy of the Boston Public Library, Print Department).

Maranville breaks a leg right at the beginning of the season, that constitutes America's greatest crisis, and if anyone reading this has to ask who Rabbit is then you should be made to show your citizenship papers." Maranville — who had been called "the Will Rogers of baseball" for his longevity, Broadway style and humorous ways — no longer had his rabbit's foot.

Maranville owed his career in the big leagues to the shrewd builder of Braves Field, Jim Gaffney. The Judge knew the story directly from Gaffney, who maintained that his team's 1914 success only stood on the deal he made in 1912, plucking Maranville up from New Bedford the first year he owned the Braves.

Gaffney had gotten word from Frank Connaughton that there was a great little player in New Bedford. By Connaughton's description, the diminutive athlete had a lot of color; in addition to speed and agility, he used those talents in combination to catch fly balls with his hands on his belt. His odd style never failed to arouse laughter and admiration.

"He never misses a catch," Connaughton, manager of the New Bedford team for the New England League, told Gaffney.

Gaffney asked his then-partner John Ward to take a run down to New Bedford to look the player over. Ward, who made no scouting report, was approached by Gaffney about Maranville in a busy Boston restaurant.

"Oh," Ward retorted. "That New Bedford player. He's no bigger than a peanut. He's too small to make good with us."

Gaffney overcame Ward's insistence that the possibility deserved no serious consideration by simply contracting for Maranville's services on the strength of Connaughton's report over his partner's. Maranville jumped at the chance to sign on with the Braves.

The Judge found Maranville considerably less excited about the mere possibility to manage the team in 1929. Maranville answered affirmatively, but only on condition of a five-year contract.

The Judge asked Maranville who told him to ask for a five-year contract.

"Driscoll told me," Maranville said, adverting to the newspaper story and his discussions as people came up to him to offer congratulations and advice.

"Driscoll?" the Judge responded. The Judge knew of the man. He told Maranville what he had heard, that Driscoll had only lasted a month as manager of the Chicago Cubs, that on his first trip to the Judge's beloved cosmopolitan New York, Driscoll had engaged a hansom cab and took the driver's seat, depositing the driver in back and driving him around town. Driscoll was not a role model, the Judge was attempting to get across.

Nonetheless, the Judge offered the job again.

Maranville declined.

There was no more said about Maranville managing, in or out of the newspapers, and the Judge stuck to the job to the end of the 1929 season. Adams, whose suggestion that the Judge manage was made partly, if not entirely, on the basis of saving money, would offer no loan for an outside manager. The Judge made do.

His season as manager has been memorialized in anecdotes, many apocryphal. When "Professor" Mel Allen spoke at the Judge's 80th birthday testimonial, he ended his humorous "question-and-answer" format with the killer:

Q: What is your opinion of Judge Fuchs as a major league manager?
A: This is his party, let him enjoy himself.

But there is also the true story of the Judge wishing a young reporter good-bye when he asked for some funny stories of the year he managed the Braves. The Judge took the job seriously. He wanted to succeed. For some period, he did succeed. Succeeding, he designated a successor but after that did not work out, the season went bad in his hands under his charge.

The very advantages that the Judge took to court to woo a jury, an unworried confidence, which stood by his ownership years of a team in trouble, were his disadvantages as manager. An unworried baseball manager is a contradiction in terms. Probably — except for the Judge in 1929 — an unworried baseball manager never existed in the major leagues. A manager's inability or disinclination to worry is an insurmountable obstacle. The Judge walked a sort of tightrope throughout 1929 between caring about his team (which he did) and not worrying about anything (which he did not). Stories reflecting any supposed ignorance of the game or indifference to strategy mean very little. The Judge tried. The team initially responded but finally did not. Had Rabbit Maranville not ducked the call to arms, the Judge would have quit, having saved some money, brought the team up right to the top, and established himself as a manager with a fantastic record. But he could not pass the torch and he ran into dilemmas: not in uniform, he could not go out on the field; an owner serving on the umpire committee, he was averse to protesting umpire's calls to avoid the appearance of impropriety.

The Judge was working hard on law cases in New York, trying (literally) to come up with the money he needed to buy good players. The conflict between his law office needs and team needs was a strike against any possibility of continuous success in either endeavor.

The Judge heard from friends, including Joe McCarthy (then himself ready to manage again, having been succeeded in Chicago by Hornsby) and John McGraw (who probably had someone in mind, if asked), that the job was a full-time one, and nothing he could do with all of his functions as the active partner-owner of the team and its public promoter.

The Judge also served on the executive committee of the National League, which hired and fired umpires. He hesitated to protest calls in the shadow of that potential conflict.

The conflict was most immediately manifest to him from an incident involving Fred McGuire. McGuire, in an away game, hit a ball between first and second and, though safe at first, was called out. The fans and press went wild, as the call was crucial to the game. When the Judge sent a clipping of the game, including the reported bad call, to league president John Heydler, Heydler looked into it. His investigation of impartial witnesses and reporters authenticated that the player, safe by a wide margin, was incorrectly called out at a crucial phase of the game. Heydler fired the umpire, and the Judge felt remorse.

The Judge hated to hide his sense of outrage over poor calls and had never run into that obstacle before as owner but now, wearing the manager's hat temporarily, he felt burdened by his permanent responsibilities in overseeing umpires and having a heavy say in their tenure as umpires.

When something similar happened in Philadelphia, when the umpire was calling "balls" that were actually fair pitches — the Judge receiving bench protests from both pitcher Bob Smith and catcher Zach Taylor — and the Judge lodged no protest, he spoke with the Philly club president, Bill Baker.

Baker, acknowledging the poor calls, admitted to the Judge that he wanted to win every game that he could but, if the Judge wanted to protest the umpire's calls to Heydler, Baker would join in that protest!

The umpire happened to seek his exit from the park through the room in which the two stood talking and offered his sympathy: "I am sorry you had to lose that kind of a ball game after being ahead."

It set the Judge off to hear sympathy from the lips of his torturer and he told the umpire, "I have no desire to discuss the matter with you but if you are an umpire tomorrow, I'll not only quit the bench, I'll sell the ball club rather than undergo the handicap of not being able to make my protest."

The Judge felt that interceding during the game was on a par with coaching a witness on the stand, and he reserved his discussion and "appeal" for afterward. It was an uncomfortable position for him, as it was personal to him, a handicap that hurt the team's chances in winning games.

The Judge relied heavily on Johnny Evers, styled "assistant manager," to produce results on the field and to make protests after that, using his best judgment.

One of the most poignant moments in the Judge's career in baseball arose early during his brief season as team manager, when he selected Eddie Brandt to pitch.

Although the Braves were doing well their first month in 1929, Brandt, a southpaw, seemed troubled. He hesitated before getting up to go warm up. The Judge noticed and grew concerned.

"Something wrong with your arm, Ed?"

"No," was the brief reply, and the pitcher walked away, but slowly. The Judge was certain that there was something the matter but, when he checked the book to be certain of time off and rotation, the Judge confirmed that it was time for Brandt to take his place on the mound.

When the Braves went out onto the field the Judge watched Brandt go over to the great first baseman, George Sisler. The year before the Judge's year as manager — the Hornsby season — Sisler had a batting average of .340. Richbourg was not far behind with .337. Hornsby's .387 topped everybody in the National League. It was a year Boston Braves counted for half of the six league leaders in batting averages — and came in seventh out of eight teams. Sisler well knew the Braves' weakness was basically in pitching at that time. Sisler, obtained for $15,000 from the Washington Senators, had proven his value many times over since joining the team. He was a trusted and steadying influence for younger players, a living legend for some of them. A member of the Braves from 1928–1930, Sisler batted .328, joining Rogers Hornsby and Lance Richbourg among the top five batters in the National League in 1928. He had a lifetime average of .340.

As noted by Gary Caruso, in his *Braves Encyclopedia,* he was called the "smartest hitter that ever lived" by Branch Rickey, and the nearest thing to a perfect player by Ty Cobb. An excellent defensive player, he batted over .300 in each of his three years with the Braves, serving as player-coach. Sisler was patient and popular with younger players.

As the Judge looked on, Sisler gave Brandt an encouraging pat on the back and the pitcher turned and headed to his assignment.

The game started. The pitcher was all too plainly nervous.

Given the batting order, the Judge could not understand it. There was nobody terrifying coming up to the plate. Incredibly, then, Brandt walked the first three hitters. They only had to stand there, so perhaps it would be better to call them the first three standees.

The Judge signaled to the bullpen for another pitcher to warm up and, being a manager not in uniform, he was unable to go out onto the field to talk with Brandt, who was instead approached by Sisler.

In a few minutes Brandt started to pitch well, striking out two, but a double scored three runs before the third man was retired.

The team came in. Sisler sidled over to the Judge and told him the story.

Brandt did not want the Judge to think he was a quitter, so he started the game, but he could not forget something that happened the night before: someone tried to bribe him, offering a thousand dollars through his beautiful girlfriend if he would throw the game. Brandt had told Sisler on the field.

The Judge called Brandt over. "Ed, I have complete faith in your honesty and ability. I will not relieve you. Stay right in there and you will win this game."

The pitcher said little more than thanks, accepting the responsibility to do his all.

The matter was investigated shortly afterward by Commissioner Landis at the Judge's instigation. (The Judge wanted to expose the gambler behind the bribe.)

"Was the gambler prosecuted?" the commissioner asked.

The Judge reported that District Attorney Foley found no criminal law in Massachusetts covered such a bribe as an unlawful act. There had been no prosecution.

The commissioner, meeting with Brandt, directed a final question to the young pitcher.

"What happened to the beautiful girl?"

"I lost the girl, commissioner, and I got even with that gambler: *I won that game!*"

Indeed, he had won more. He won a secure place in the Judge's list of people who made the game of baseball "honest and great."

The Boston Braves were not without talent during their last-place 1928 and 1929 seasons. For example, anyone at Braves Field on June 2, 1928, witnessed something incredible. Otherwise unknown Les Bell hit three homers and narrowly missed a fourth in that one game. On May 10, 1929, as the Judge's team was just beginning its slide from first place, Earl Clark set a league record of 12 putouts in one game. There were bright moments of promise, stars in a dark night.

10

The Scribes, the Tribe and the Judge

"Old Boze Bulger once declared that during his more than twenty years as a baseball writer he had never known a man connected with the game that came up to Judge Fuchs for real, honest kindness. It was not what the Judge did for you so much as the way he did it that won your heart."
— Sports columnist Cullen Cain (1948)

In Boston in the twenties, sports writers were "scribes" while the "Tribe" was the Braves. Judge Fuchs presided at and issued press releases from Braves Field, the "Wigwam." Having few tribal glories to memorialize during the twenties and thirties, besides dry reports of Braves games, reporters sketched the Judge and his lifestyle; indeed, the scribes were part of that lifestyle.

Austen Lake termed the Judge's generosity "almost psychopathic." As a young reporter with the Boston *Record-American*, he had been astounded to witness the Judge's feasts for "whole hotelsful of people."

"The only thing the Judge loved better than giving a dinner was giving two dinners," the writer concluded. He also recalled the Judge's unsuccessful effort to suppress a story. When a detective confirmed suspicions that an employee was turning back the turnstiles after games to reduce the numbers of paid admissions to provide a difference which he pocketed (thousands of dollars a season), the Judge met with Lake and other reporters.

"Now, this fellow was pretty good to you boys," the Judge said of the employee, who had been generous to the press, too—with Braves' money! The Judge had fished a gun from out of the employee's coat during the confrontation over the missing funds. The Judge was concerned for the man and his family. His request to the reporters was, "Don't write anything that might drive him to a rash act!"

The Judge's request was ignored, and stories appeared.

But the Judge's rapport was continuous and unbroken, especially with their most senior member, chief of scribes at that time, James "Uncle Jim" O'Leary. O'Leary was himself given a surprise party one spring training night down in Florida, attended by members of the cabinet and movie stars. It was only fitting as O'Leary headed the "Wigwam Cabinet" or "Brain Trust" to whom the Judge looked for advice and help. For one example, O'Leary good-naturedly adorned his bald head with a ten-gallon cowboy hat sent by Tom Mix, undertaking a job as the volunteer head of a publicity team for a Braves–Red Sox game held to benefit the unemployed in 1933. When Babe Ruth signed his contract at the Wigwam in February 1935, O'Leary, Chief of Scribes, was on hand to sign as a witness. Together with O'Leary, the Judge sought out the opinions of Burt Whitman of the *Herald*, Paul Shannon of the *Post* and Nick Flatley of the *American*. These men had a virtual veto power on Braves hirings and firings, so great was the Judge's confidence in their judgment. Almost ten years after the Judge had picked Bill McKechnie to succeed the Judge as the team's manager, Sam Breadon recalled the event with bemused laughter. John Drohan was moved to write the Judge. He had been attending the 1937 World Series on assignment for the *Herald-Traveler*. He wrote:

> Sam Breadon brought up your name and told of the time he induced you to take Bill McKechnie as your manager at the 1929 World Series. Sam laughed as he related how you said, "The Boston writers won't go for him."
> Then he said, "Let me talk to them." Sam described how he proceeded to sell them McKechnie and when it got through, he was nearly floored "when that little fellow with a twist to his mouth"—Nick Flatley—said, "Well, if he's so good, why are you giving him to us?"

Breadon was still laughing, years later. (The full story is told in the next chapter.) The Judge at least once gave advice the scribes themselves needed and followed: He suggested that they establish a Boston chapter of the Baseball Writers' Association. He even contributed start-up costs by throwing them their first dinner. The chapter still exists and, at annual dinners, memorializes the Judge by giving the top award to a person who has given long and meritorious service to baseball. (A complete list of winners of the Judge Fuchs Award is included in Appendix C.)

The Judge's chief assistant and all-around team administrator beginning in the mid-twenties, Eddy Cunningham, was a scribe selected for the

Judge by the scribes when he asked them to find him someone who could best help him. The Judge's business and social lives merged in hundreds of informal get-togethers, formal dinners, bridge parties and song fests, hosting the scribes. The Judge would separate the bridge players, identifying with his expertise those whom he assigned to the "minor league" table while others he placed in the "major league." He and Eddy Cunningham would keep the sandwiches and beverages coming, sometimes until dawn. It was not unusual for a columnist like Bill Cunningham to be pounding out ragtime after midnight at the Copley-Plaza Hotel while the Judge organized others into quartets. (Austen Lake recalled the night the Judge lost a wealthy client, Colonel Guggenheim, of the famed Guggenheim Foundation, by refusing to interrupt a song to take a call about a case on appeal in New York's top court.) One reporter recalled the period as "his front seat on the roller-coaster." At the scribes' first dinner, given by the Judge, his dour partner was the butt of a joke. Seizing on the name he shared with a prominent official, Bill Cunningham quipped in mock disappointment that he had "come to meet the Secretary of the Navy and all I meet is my grocer." He played the piano for the grocer, the Judge and his fellow scribes until 3 A.M.

The Judge kept his contacts with the scribes after 1935. Serving during wartime as a sports writer, he never lacked for a seat in the press box at either Braves Field or Fenway Park. Later generations of reporters found him good for a quote or feature, often running the Judge's opinions on baseball issues as news items. In July 1957, for example, the Boston *Traveler*'s Tim Horgan sought out the Judge's opinion on the reserve clause, which was under investigation in Congress. Headlined "Toss Out the Reserve Clause: Fuchs," Horgan's article carried the Judge's prophetic warning to owners that they had best reform, reducing it to a limited period or baseball "would be fated to end up like the roller derby."

Sam Brogna, now treasurer of the Boston chapter of the scribes' association, covered the Red Sox for many years from the Fenway Park press box, where he and the Judge's black cigars became familiar. It was on the basis of his trademark cigar and cane that the Judge broke into the widely-read syndicated "Ripley's 'Believe It or Not'" cartoon: an envelope with no other address than Jamaica Plain, Boston, under a sketch of a cane and a cigar was delivered, as intended by its sender, to the Judge!

But less caricature and more character, the Judge was a beloved and legendary baseball owner in his own time. He preferred to think that the scribes knew baseball better than he did. (Just as he claimed always to be a poor businessman.) But maintaining ownership of a major league team for over 12 years while never clinching a pennant and coveting the cellar most seasons, the Judge had to have something not only of baseball savvy but also business ability. In this connection it is noteworthy that the Judge's tenure was marked by the Great Depression, no Sunday baseball, no night baseball and no television proceeds. The Judge's typical approach was simply one of modest politeness. His affable and compassionate attitude was not lost on Braves players, fans or on those who associated with him most closely and, ultimately, knew him best: the Scribes of the Tribe of the Wigwam.

11

The Scribes
Elect McKechnie

"Of all recipients of the Judge Fuchs Award, Bill McKechnie appeared to be the most moved. When he came up to the mike to speak, he just couldn't. He was tearful. He apologized, but I didn't think apologies were in order. It was a great tribute, those tears. He kept the award until he died, and then he willed it to the Baseball Hall of Fame. But then, my father thought quite a lot of Bill McKechnie, too. It was a mutual respect and closeness. They went through the best and worst years that the Braves had between the wars, the most promising and profitable, and the worst of all, the year my father lost the Braves, 1935. McKechnie was there."
— Bob Fuchs (1995)

Braves "headquarters" during a World Series was popular with Boston sports writers. Few covering the games were old enough to have reported on the Boston Braves in a World Series — by 1929 it had been 15 years since that event — but for years the Judge had provided something for their appetites and such entertainments as singing and card playing. In Chicago one night in 1929 the Judge hosted the men known as "scribes" with a more serious purpose.

"The Braves were looking for a new manager," the Judge wrote of his situation many years later. "I knew of no better place to look over the field and get various opinions than at a World Series, when all of the men of baseball who possibly can get there are to be found in the lobbies of the leading hotels."

But the Judge abandoned searching for talent in hotel lobbies and cornered Boston's sportswriters at his hotel suite during the Series between the Cubs and the Athletics.

"I told them what I wanted to do," he recalled. "I outlined the history of my ownership, during which we'd had four managers."

He described Fred Mitchell to them as "deliberate and loyal," Dave Bancroft as a "colorful, talented, quick-thinking type," Jack Slattery, "the veteran expert of the game," and Rogers Hornsby "that frank, devoted and often misunderstood fighting-hitting leader." He omitted numbering himself as the team's fifth manager. Instead, he reproved himself for having served simultaneously as both president and manager of a major league club. Then he got to his real point: he wanted the scribes' best advice at this time of team crisis, their help in selecting the next manager of the Boston Braves.

What did the scribes think of Bill McKechnie? He was a possibility.

The Judge had just been closeted with Sam Breadon, owner of the Cardinals. For over two hours they had discussed the prospect of Breadon's manager, McKechnie, going from St. Louis to Boston. But, given the obvious question, why the owner of the Cardinals would part with his manager, the Judge sought to think out loud and to have input from people who not only knew baseball but who knew and cared about the Boston Braves.

The Judge explained that McKechnie had started the 1929 season as manager of the Cardinals' farm team, which played in Rochester. At midseason Billy Southworth had gone to Rochester while McKechnie had been brought up to replace him as manager of the Cardinals. St. Louis, which had invented the farm team system, made use of it as a developing ground for its managers as well as its players.

After the Boston writers discussed the possibility, their prejudice was made visible through a secret ballot: not one was marked for McKechnie.

The Judge, veteran of a thousand matches of advocacy in the courtroom, turned the session into a confrontation between the writers who had just voted and Sam Breadon, who had recommended McKechnie. Breadon was invited in to hear their reasons for opposing McKechnie's coming to Boston and, if he could, to respond.

"Our first question will floor him, Judge," one of the writers asserted with a confidence that reflected the feelings of the entire knowledgeable group. The scribes were certain of their view.

"I will be satisfied if you feel the same way about this after listening to Sam," the Judge replied.

When Breadon came into the room the "first question" boasted of was sprung: "If you think so much of McKechnie and of his ability as a major league manager, why don't you have him stay on to manage the Cardinals in 1930?"

The question did not stump the speaker; Breadon had to have anticipated it and answered at length with no hesitation.

"I'm glad that you boys asked that question," he said, warming to the
subject, welcoming it as first pitch. "St. Louis is one of the smaller cities
in the National League. In order to make money there we must win the pennant or at least be a contender all season, each season. When a manager,
no matter how good he is, does not win, then we are forced by our fans to
make a change."

The economic side of the matter had escaped the writers' attention
but it was a credible point. St. Louis did not have the margin that Boston
did to wait for a team to develop. Having managed the team for half a season and that season finishing fourth among National League teams,
McKechnie had to go. What Breadon said made sense to the scribes.

Breadon extolled McKechnie's talent as "one of the best handlers of
pitchers" he had ever seen and — more importantly, for the Boston Braves —
"the best man available to build up a ball club." McKechnie, fondly known
as the "Deacon," exhibited patience and natural "fatherly" interest in players, which had made him a key figure in the team's farm system and were
strong points of appeal for the Boston team which, in baseball terms, was
a farm team playing in a major league stadium.

For another two hours Breadon fielded questions from all comers. The
scribes eventually caught onto the problem Boston faced, which had been
familiar to McKechnie, whereby his special assets could be exactly what the
Braves needed to come up out of the cellar, to become a contending team,
to break into the first division, to see a pennant fly over Braves Field in the
1930s.

As promised, the Judge sought a second vote after Breadon left.

The next ballot was as unanimous as had been the first — but it was
unanimously in favor of McKechnie as the first had been unanimously
opposed.

With the support of the scribes assembled in his hotel suite at the
Chicago World Series game, the Judge made the arrangements with Breadon
by which McKechnie became the new manager of the Boston Braves, with
his mission a clear one: to bring a farm team up into the major leagues, to
become contenders.

McKechnie was especially good at developing pitchers. Once the Braves
had assembled a pitching staff (as they did by 1932) and they had a few
power hitters (primarily, Wally Berger and Randy Moore), the team was in
contention for a flag. Wally Berger's 38 home runs in 1930 constituted not
only a new record for rookies but stood as the best home run record of the

1930 season. A new Babe Ruth seemed to be coming to life in Boston. The Braves' overall play was correspondingly better.

By 1932 the team's earned run average — an ERA earned largely within the cavernous (though remodeled) Braves Field — was second only to the World Series–winning Cubs. Its break-even season (77–77) was its best finish since the Judge took over. Its pitching roster included five ten-game winners. Within a month of opening day in 1932, people were excited about possibilities. A crowd of 51, 531 filled Braves Field on May 22, 1932, for a doubleheader against the 1929 and 1930 champs and 1931 World Series losers (by one game), Connie Mack's Philadelphia Athletics. Fans were wild about the team, sensing opportunity with unusual prescience. Their team did not disappoint them against the three-time pennant winners; the Braves took the first game 4–2 and narrowly lost the second game 5–3 in the tenth inning. The whole season they remained competitive. Ironically — by one game! — the Athletics secured fourth place, First Division rights on a record of 78 wins and 76 losses. The Braves came next by having won exactly half (77) of their games and standing at the threshold of the First Division the team would break through the next year at last.

In 1933, the Braves ranked second after the Giants in early September. If the Braves had beaten the Giants in the games scheduled, the Braves would have been number one. The same enthusiasm and hope filling the stadium in the spring of 1932 overfilled, spilling over into the streets in the late summer of 1933.

McKechnie's pitcher development forte invites a "what if" question: What if the Boston Braves had moved Johnny VanderMeer up from its farm club in 1935 instead of bringing Babe Ruth up from the Yankees?

Bob Fuchs had a hand in the pitcher's elevation from the farm to the show. Bob described it:

> Scranton was in town, playing the Harrisburg team. I ran into the Scranton team's accountant at the local beanery. We shared a table to talk baseball. He turned out to be a fan so crazy about baseball that he traveled with the team at his own expense. He made it a point to keep up with all of the players, their skills, their habits, their potential.
>
> He identified a pitcher who did not smoke or drink as having what he called "all the stuff in the world but very wild."
>
> I thought of Bill McKechnie as the greatest manager of pitchers in the game. We both agreed, McKechnie could straighten the kid out. The next day, before our game, the accountant brought young VanderMeer over to meet me. After our chat, I watched him pitch. He did have "stuff" — and he was wild, too. That night I called Boston and my scouting report bore fruit. Despite the Depression and low gate at Braves Field, they came up with $1,500 to buy VanderMeer's Scranton contract.

Of course, it was just too late in the game.

After the Judge lost the team, which was shortly after Johnny Vander-Meer's contract was purchased, he was traded for a veteran Brooklyn pitcher. Well, he broke a strikeout record for rookie pitchers, but not wearing a Boston Braves uniform after all. Ironically, Bill McKechnie later obtained him for the Cincinnati club when Bill was managing the Reds — for a $30,000 price, as I recall.

Ed Brandt is a good example of McKechnie's influence. In 1928, Brandt was the "losingest" pitcher in the National League with 9 wins and 21 losses. He scarcely improved in 1929 or 1930. With McKechnie's patient coaching and avuncular concern, Brandt began to break records, turning around the win-loss ratio. He was 18– in 1931, 16–16 in 1932, 18–14 in 1933 and 16–14 in 1934. Brandt became a consistent pitcher with a winning record. The manager of the early thirties deserves credit: Bill McKechnie.

McKechnie, still the only person to manage three different ball clubs in the World Series, was a fundamentalist who believed in strong, defensive play. The Judge deserves credit for determining that Braves Field's made-for-defense contours and his "needs work" ball club would be the perfect match for the patient and defense-focused McKechnie. It was a marriage made in Heaven. The Judge and McKechnie were both gentlemanly rule-abiding sportsmen. McKechnie became a virtual part of the Fuchs family, a frequent visitor at their Jamaica Plain home. Shortly after the Judge's death, McKechnie was awarded the fourth Judge Emil Fuchs Memorial Award for Long and Meritorious Service to Baseball by the Boston Chapter of the Baseball Writers' Association of America. A few words into his acceptance speech, he became too choked up and apologized instead, saying he could not go on with it. A generation after they had severed their owner-manager relationship (a relationship tried that final year by Babe Ruth, a team slump and no cash), McKechnie's memories of the Judge were affectionate.

The Judge vividly recalled the Braves as neck-and-neck rivals with the Giants for the flag in September 1933:

> We won the first game and tied one out of four doubleheaders. Eight games in all were played to a capacity crowd. The series demonstrated that, when fans were begging to buy tickets at a premium, nothing succeeds like success on the field.
>
> I recall the night before the first game bleacher tickets went on sale at 9 A.M. Many fans slept outside Braves Field to get in line to get their tickets. I arranged with the armory across the street to allow them to stay over in their order of arrival. And we opened sales at 8 A.M., admitting first those from the armory. Gaffney Street was so crowded before game time

that I had to request police officers to see that dignitaries like former Boston Mayor John F. Fitzgerald and others could get through unimpeded. I met Mayor Fitzgerald and an entourage of priests in the street, to help see them through to their seats.

Randy Moore, one of our most successful hitters, was hit by a pitched ball in the thumb, which disabled him for the rest of the season. I paid the Washington club $25,000 for a player by the name of Thompson, hoping that he might take Randy's place for the rest of the games and we might stay in contending position. Although Thompson was a fairly good player, he could not take Randy's place. Randy had won many a game for us at crucial turning points.

The Judge, of course, watched the game with heightened interest:

> I was sitting in the bleachers with Sidney Rabb, who headed the Stop & Shop supermarket chain. Sidney was not only a stockholder of the Braves but also a close personal friend.
>
> In the last part of the game, the Braves were behind.
>
> With bases loaded, McKechnie called upon Wally Berger. Berger, though one of our great hitters, had had a severe cold but that day put on his uniform and an overcoat, suffering from a fever with a temperature of 102.
>
> Nonetheless, he took the first pitch and hit it into the bleachers for a home run.
>
> I was among many who cheered without restraint, taking my cane and hat and waving them around with enthusiasm.

Massachusetts Governor Ely is set to throw out the first ball of the 1934 season (courtesy of the Boston Public Library, Print Department).

Afterward, Sidney said to me, "Judge, you are a baseball fan but a bad business man. Don't you know that that hit of Berger's meant that you finished in the first division and that hit will cost you $5,000?"

He knew, of course, about a clause in our contract with McKechnie, providing him with a nice bonus if the team finished in the first division.

The Judge could only smile and refer Sidney to the thrill of it.

As things turned out, that last game of the 1933 season was the climax, after which it was all downhill. He shared his finest hour with Sidney Rabb watching Wally Berger hit a home run that cost him. It was an expensive thrill, as were really all of the years of his ownership. But the Judge regretted not a bit of it.

In 1934, though never so close to the pennant, the Braves took aim — in the last game of the season — to finish for a second consecutive time in the First Division.

As in 1923, in 1934 the Braves' National League standing was at stake in the last day, and they were in a doubleheader. But in 1923 the Braves had been fighting Philadelphia over the last-place honors. In 1934 the Braves teetered on the edge of their second consecutive First Division finish, as fourth team of the league, in for a cut of the World Series' action and to be deemed a competitive team. The same player who had hit a dramatic homer to clinch fourth place in 1933, when he had been ill, Wally Berger, can be credited with saving the game and the season again in 1934. In the tenth inning of the first game against Philadelphia, Berger's double followed by power hitter Randy Moore's single gave the Braves a 4–3 victory over Philadelphia. The next game, called after seven innings, was also won by Ed Brandt and the Braves, 5 to 4.

Bill McKechnie and his Boston Braves had answered the fans' expectations as satisfactorily as Sam Breadon had answered the scribes'.

12

The Spohrer-Shires Fight of 1930

"Spohrer talked so convincingly that many of the boys were ready to back him to the limit."

— Judge Fuchs on the team's
offseason betting opportunity
at the Boston Garden (1930)

The Boston Braves' 169-pound catcher, Al Spohrer, hoped to make some money. His wife was always hounding him for money and the pay he got for squatting behind the plate at Braves Field did not match his own financial ambitions. He thought that one way to increase his income during the offseason would be by boxing in the then-new Boston Garden (open just over a year).

But against whom could he fight? Certainly, he was no match for a professional boxer. David found his Goliath in Chicago White Sox first baseman Art Shires, the 175-pound winner of three of his fights by knockouts who claimed to be the "Champion Boxer of Baseball." A Boston boxing promoter, Eddie Mack, played matchmaker.

The Judge describes the situation not resolved until a confrontation at the Boston Garden on January 10, 1930:

> Shires had engaged in a few boxing bouts previous to coming to Boston and had been successful. He lost no time in spreading the glory of his accomplishments. Spohrer was not convinced. He intimated that Shires had been boxing with some setups and, on various occasions, let the Great Shires know that he did not have any great respect for Art's talents inside the ropes.
>
> This difference of opinion naturally built up a keen rivalry between the

89

two and Eddie Mack, the boxing promoter, got wind of the situation. It looked like a natural and it was arranged to have the two settle the rivalry with gloves at the Boston Garden.

Both began to train seriously. Spohrer told some of his playmates that he had boxed frequently with Tommy Loughran in Philadelphia and that the talented Tommy never had been able to lay a glove on him.

Spohrer talked so convincingly that many of the boys were ready to back him to the limit. Word of Spohrer's phantom-like sparring ability reached Shires and must have made an impression because he was not so bullish in saying what he would do to Al.

Spohrer told Shires to get a couple of former heavyweight champions as his seconds, and as many others as he desired, but only one second would handle Spohrer and he was none less than that veteran handler of men, the widely known V. C. Bruce Wetmore.

Two nights before the bout Spohrer came to me and said, "My honor is at stake. I have just been down to Commissioner of Police Crowley to lodge a complaint that someone, and I believe he was connected with Shires' backers, offered me a bribe of $5,000 to lay down in the fight and spare Art the humiliation of knocking him out."

Spohrer was all steamed up over this, but cooled down when his able trainer Bruce Wetmore said, "Al, your decisive victory will be your answer to this insult."

The night of the big bout arrived. One of the largest crowds that ever attended a boxing bout indoors in Boston jammed the Garden. The fans literally were hanging from the rafter.

The Great Shires came down the aisle accompanied by seven seconds, who surrounded him in his corner. Spohrer was escorted only by Wetmore, who was clad in a heavy fur coat and wore a tall hat. Bruce also carried the pail, sponge, bottle and towel.

Turning to Bruce in his corner Spohrer said, "Bruce, they have all the seconds, but we have all the style. Those seven men will come in handy carrying Shires out of the Garden when I get through with him."

Bruce agreed with Spohrer that it was only a question of time when the procession would start from the opposite corner and wend its way slowly to the dressing room of the Great Shires, who would be great no longer.

The gong sounded. The grim gladiators felt each other out for about two seconds, each looking for those weak spots. Then Shires led with his right, the blow landing squarely on the top of Spohrer's bald head and down he went.

Al was on his feet at the count of eight but it seemed that he got up sort of reluctantly. Apparently the canvas had felt like a downy couch and had urged him to repose there.

Then Spohrer started doing some fancy footwork, trying to tire out Shires. Al lifted the tempo and soon was flying around the ring, with Shires vainly trying to catch up with him.

Wetmore also was flying but in a different direction. He was setting a new speed record getting out of the Garden. He went so fast that his fur coat had a tough time keeping up with him.

Spohrer's wife, the inspiration of the 1930 fight, always went to the headquarters waiting for his check on payday — and a sympathetic management would slip it to him and Danny Donnahue, police officer with a motorcycle and sidecar, would whip Al to the South Station when the team went on the road. Spohrer finally resolved his domestic situation in keeping with being a man who believed in baseball's traditions. When playing in Scranton in the New York–Pennsylvania League he traded his wife for the wife of the second baseman — and got the worst of the deal.

Two years later Shires was traded to Boston.

On reporting for spring training at the Braves' St. Petersburg camp, Shires placed his items in the veteran Spohrer's locker, staking his claim further with a note on the locker door:

"I knocked you on your ass in Boston and now claim all rights, title and interest in your locker."

There was no fight over the locker between the two.

It was one case of Goliath beating the hell out of David!

13

The "Knot Hole Gang"

"The building's architecture resembled a giant stucco-house with gable-like gate entrances. Inside, practically everything was made of wood and painted dark green. There was a section of the bleachers in right field shaped like a jury box for which it was aptly named. The grandstand seats were painted green slats and were very comfortable...The scene was tranquil in spite of all the activity..."

— Harriet Tirrell Nemiccolo
describing Braves Field in the 1930s

It is small, 2¼ inches by 4 inches, made of thin cardboard and colored green. More than 50 years later, it is still with its owner, Philip Gates, whose name is penned in as being "a regular member of the Braves Knot Hole Gang," with the registration number PN-157.

Such cards, issued by YMCAs and city recreation agencies in the Boston area, were boys' most precious possessions in the twenties and thirties.

"Always Take This Card to the Game," their cards stated. With the card and a nickel, a Knot Hole Gang member would have a seat over in the third base pavilion near left field, where the bullpen crews warmed up before and during the games. The cards were passports for thousands of youngsters at a time of tight family budgets. With the Knot Hole Gang, they saw big league action.

For one nickel Philip Gates saw something he remembered the rest of his life.

"I remember Wally Berger," he said, "hitting the grand slam in the final game of the 1933 season, which lifted the Braves into the First Division! Unheard of heights!"

It was, indeed. The home run, the game, the first season during the

Judge's ownership that the Braves scaled the height of First Division, and its best season — 83 wins, 71 losses. With their team finally winning, Knot Holers aspired to keep it that way. With their assigned seats fronting the bullpen, their attention was often on pitchers.

"Huck Betts had three pitches — slow, slower and slowest," Philip Gates reported. "Spohrer had a hell of an arm and used to fire the ball back at Betts so hard that we all yelled, 'Let Spohrer pitch!'"

Philip Gates's aspiration did not cease with rooting for Spohrer to pitch. He was a fan of the first order: the first ticket buyer at Fenway Park after its 1934 renovation, he later designed the boxscore format used in newspapers today, having submitted it by a letter to columnist Bill Cunningham. Although he remembers characters such as "Shanty" Hogan ("built like an Irish shanty and slow as cold molasses"), Baxter Jordan and what he recalls as an outstanding outfield (Schulmerich, Berger and Worthington), he has no hesitation in saying that Wally Berger was the big star. He noted this, notwithstanding having observed the Rabbit Maranville unique "vest pocket" catches of infield flies.

Lester Smith is another Knot Holer. Smith, who grew up in Chelsea, similarly recalled how the "gang" would "sit in the third base stands and watch what were, in fact, pretty terrible baseball teams."

But the boys would root for the Braves players anyway.

"We'd see Kurt Greenfield or Socks Siebold or Ed Brandt try, desperately, to win an occasional ball game," he said, while noting with gratitude that "at least Wally Berger hit home runs."

Years later Smith worked as a sportscaster with WNAC on radio and television, including some play-by-play announcing of Braves games. Although not all Knot Holers went on to do anything in professional baseball, most say, as Smith does, "The important thing was that we saw big league baseball for the price of the streetcar from home to Braves Field and back."

Many of the boys arrived at games with a sandwich or crackers and something to drink, being unable to raise more than the nickel for admission to the park. Besides games and skillful offense or defense which still come to mind when Braves Field or the Boston Braves are mentioned, these boys remember brief exchanges between themselves and players in or around the bullpen. The Braves were friendly with the youngsters and would sometimes autograph a piece of paper or a ball.

Some Knot Holers never let go of their memories. Their sons and daughters inherited vicarious experiences. For example, Kenneth Portnoy of Marblehead, Massachusetts, knows of his father's rollerskating with friends up the Esplanade and Commonwealth Avenue for what his old man always called "one of the great pleasures of his youth," watching the Braves with the Knot Holers. In his possession still is his father's worn 1927 copy of *Balldom*, with complete statistics on teams of that year, the Braves' figures highlighted.

One Knot Holer never let go of his memory of "crime" at the ballpark. Daniel Leavitt, these days of Boca Raton, Florida, when 12 or 13 years old took his ride from his Mattapan home on the street car to Egleston Square, then the elevated train to Summer Street station, followed by a short run on the subway at Washington station to Park Street station, from which he joined the crowds on the long combination underground-surface street car trip to Braves Field off Commonwealth Avenue. Entering for his nickel, having displayed his Knot Hole Gang card, he took his place in the appropriate third base pavilion. Attendance was low; after an inning, Leavitt and company sneaked into the grandstand. These seats ("with backs") were a dollar. Leavitt sent a letter to the authors along with a check for 95 cents to rectify his Braves Field "wrong." (He was given absolution for free, for his confession and anecdote.)

William G. "John" Grinnell, a three-letter athlete at Tufts, was a Knot Holer.

"I didn't know there was such a thing as the Red Sox. I mean that literally: as far as I knew growing up, there was only the Braves. I don't know how old I was before I learned that there was any other team in Boston."

Grinnell's first cousin, 8 years older, Clyde Sukeforth, was a catcher with the Cincinnati Reds.

"When Cincinnati was in town Clyde would always visit with his people in Somerville and we'd meet. I remember going with Clyde to Braves Field in 1928. Rogers Hornsby was player-manager that season for the club. I asked Clyde, 'How do you pitch to Hornsby?'

"He said, 'Hornsby has no identified weakness. You just move the ball around.'"

Grinnell recalled pitcher Burleigh Grimes (later a Hall of Famer) and "a second-baseman named Moriarty" as especially good.

"I wasn't a Knot Holer by the time of Wally Berger," Grinnell said. "To see him I paid full fare. But he was a thrill to watch. He was worth the ticket even without the discount."

Another Knot Holer, Ed Spargo of Quincy, Massachusetts, continues to regale people with stories of games in which all of the players have died and most of the audience. He is a crusader for healthful living and his longevity, as he reaches 90, is "living proof" that he has a store of practical tips.

"Every Saturday Braves Field was home for us kiddoes," Spargo, a reporter and retired editor for Quincy newspapers, wrote.

"Judge Fuchs let us in for a nickel, the best bargain in Beantown," he said. Spargo, who saw Babe Ruth in a Red Sox uniform when he was taken to his first game at Fenway Park, was an astute judge of the difference between what he saw at Braves Field and what he saw at Fenway.

"When the national pastime was introduced the object was to manufacture one run at a time. The Braves were past masters at that art. Whereas, in Fenway, everyone swung for the fences as they bypassed strategy in favor of the long ball — home runs," Spargo said. He appreciated the "finesse" offered by Braves players in their large park. Spargo observed and analyzed much later what he thinks is one of the greatest feats of the game. In 1928 Rogers Hornsby, a player-manager of a "low-market" club, struggling with all the headaches of both positions, batted an amazing .387 and slugging average of .632.

"I can still see him astride the batter's box," Spargo said. "By God, he was one of the greatest. An astonishing thing: Hornsby's power was to right center. The greatest right-handed batter who ever lived."

Spargo was one of the few who did better as an adult than he had as a kid, in terms of the Braves. In the Knot Hole Gang he had to pay his nickel like everyone else. He recalled proudly that the Judge sent him four season tickets for Braves games when he became sports editor of the old *Quincy News*.

When one mentions the Braves to senior citizens, men who have become very wealthy, successful businessmen, they brighten up and warmly recall the days of the Depression when they were Knot Holers and attended the games for a nickel. Dick O'Connell received the Judge Fuchs Award in 1971. He related how his mother would give him a nickel to get in, another nickel for a drink and a sandwich and he would ride the trolley in from Revere. District Attorney Droney recalls how, when he was the first treasurer of John F. Kennedy's campaign for Congress, JFK came in with Powers and introduced them, not realizing that they were boyhood friends. They told him how they were members of the Knot Hole Gang — and in addition to going to the games together they would hide between the grandstand and the third base pavilion until it got dark and then pop up to watch boxing. Droney remarked that JFK was most envious of their boyhood adventures.

Jason Wolf — a prominent sports accountant who represented Red Auerbach personally, as well as the Celtics, to whom Tom Yawkey would send his young ball players for advice on how to invest — walked to Braves

Field all the way from Somerville to attend the games as a member of the Knot Hole Gang, not even having money for the streetcar.

They walked (or rode, if lucky) from all sections of the city, from all races and ethnic groups, to enjoy the Judge's most enduring gift, his contribution to brightening the Depression-blighted lives of children of the area: the Knot Hole Gang.

14

Home of the Braves

*"The 1932 Braves are going to be a very much improved ball club —
besides being the most colorful team since 1914."*
— Judge Fuchs on the Braves (January 21, 1932)

If Boston could be home to only one baseball team, in the thirties that team would have been the Braves. It was not the Braves but the Red Sox which was the club in trouble during the early Depression years. After expensive remodeling of Fenway Park, which was followed by a fire that gutted much of the stadium, the team simply had less fan support to fall back upon than had their National League rivals at Braves Field. This was the reverse of the trend of the twenties.

During the 1923–28 period the Red Sox outdrew the Braves handily, averaging 300,000 fans a season during which time the Braves were lucky to approach even 250,000. After 1929, the year of the Judge's own titular management of the team with able assistants (which ended in a dead heat, both the Red Sox and Braves securing records of 400,000 paid admissions each), the Braves pulled ahead of the Sox quite dramatically. The graph below shows the story in numbers:

Year	Braves	Red Sox
1930	464,835	444,045
1931	515,005	350,975
1932	507,606	182,150
1933	517,803	268,715

Attendance at Braves Field exploded in the early thirties not only by comparison to Fenway Park among Boston fans, but was increasing substantially, contrary to a national trend at a time National League admissions spiraled down from 4.6 million (1931) to 3.8 million (1932) to 3.2

million (1933) as the Depression in cities away from Boston drained dollars away from diamonds.

The Braves were business successes by local or national measures, hot stuff in a frigid economy. The Judge, who had invested heavily in the future of baseball in Boston when he underwrote costs of the referendum campaign to repeal the law against Sunday baseball, had been wise. The team that had wandered in the desert in the twenties seemed to be entering the Promised Land before and without a pennant or a World Series championship, only as a middling-record team. Certainly as a promoter, the Judge knew his business, and that business was baseball. So powerful was the spell he cast that the disastrous unemployment, soup kitchens and bread lines popping up everywhere did not hinder fans from paying tribute to their reborn team. Indeed, the bare record of paid admissions illustrates the situation. Paid admissions for the three years 1930–32, 1,487,446, very nearly equals the first six years, 1923–28, of the Judge's ownership of the Braves, 1,538,092. In 1922, the last season of G.W. Grant, paid attendance had been 167,965. In 1933 it stood at 517,803.

The years of McKechnie were pivotal to the Judge's ownership of the team. Wally Berger was brought up. Rabbit Maranville still made his patented "vest-pocket catches" to the delight of onlooking fans, some of whom had seen him with the "Miracle Braves" of 1914. The Judge's statement that his 1932 team would be next in colorful characters after 1914 had its support in fact. Although Casey Stengel had gone and would not return with the Braves until after the Judge's time, besides Berger, who swung like crazy for homers whether he hit the ball or struck out, Maranville, "Shanty" Hogan and Hall of Famer George Sisler, there were fabulous pitchers. In the early thirties, Boston was authentically "Home of the Braves." It simultaneously became the home of the Judge as he stopped commuting and moved his family to Boston. The man who had come for dinner at the Lambs Club in 1922 had decided to stay. There was no going back to New York when he owned a team that had potential. The Judge shut down his law office in New York and devoted himself fully to the Braves. Together, he and his new manager seemed to be headed for an inevitable and trend-bucking success.

For the first time it was possible to make money out of the air with a ball club. Paid admissions at the park, earlier the basic way teams made money, were still important but were soon to become less than half of team revenues. In the Judge's time, radio broadcasts of Braves games began with the sale of the first season's rights for $5,000 to the Yankee network. The program was popular. Although it was the Depression, the network agreed to jump that rate by half to $7,500 for rights to the next season. Too early for television, too early for big radio money and such franchises as teams sell today as matters of big business, the Judge enlarged team income potential to the limits of this time. He continued to seek players to develop and to risk everything on the future. He did not want to struggle along on 300,000 paid admissions a year. He wanted 400,000 or 500,000 fans to pass through the gates of Braves Field. And he came to have that dream realized 1931 through 1933, years of Wally Berger.

After 1927, when he hit 60 home runs, even Babe Ruth wasn't Babe Ruth. Was he unique or wasn't he? Kids in the bleachers, lords in the owner's boxes, gentlemen of the press hailed "new Babe Ruths" beginning in the late twenties. There wasn't enough Babe Ruth. Every team wanted one. The Boston Braves needed one. Remarkably — before he came himself, in 1935 — the Braves got their "Babe" in the form of Wally Berger.

In 1930 Wally Berger broke all previous rookie records for home runs, including Babe Ruth's. Brought up from the Pacific league by the Judge, Berger was worry-food. That is, had the Judge been inclined to worry, he would have fretted between Berger's drain on the club's meager revenues and the possibility of injury or slump in his only champion batsman. The Judge kept Berger and counted on the man in the street — Boston streets, people from Jamaica Plain, Roxbury, Charlestown, Southie — to buy tickets, Depression or no Depression, to support and to see the Berger-driven Braves. They witnessed Wally Berger's finest hours. The people wanted to see records broken, but Berger particularly wanted to break a record himself — in the salary field.

From Los Angeles after his first, wonderful season, Berger wrote the Judge, asking rhetorically, "Would you take a cent less than $10,000?" The Judge took the question and turned the figure under analysis, noting to Berger that "no second year man in the history of baseball that I know of or am able to learn of ever received a $10,000 contract for his second year's services." The Babe Ruth standard was implied: even Babe Ruth, in his second year, did not get $10,000.

Berger had made a serious mistake in asking the Judge what he himself would do. The Judge answered at length. "Your mention in your letter what I would do if I were in your position. Inasmuch as you make that statement I will answer it — if I were in your position, having in mind your youth and physical ability, I would sign the contract, say nothing more about it, remain the same modest young man that you have been, and demonstrate your right to the same consideration next year that you have received this."

Berger's salaries from the Judge were as follows: 1930 — $4,000; 1931 — $8,500; 1932 — $10,000; 1933 — $10,000; 1934 — $11,500; 1935 — $12,500. (The 1933 figure of $10,000 was an afterthought. Everyone on the team, including its owner, the Judge, took a cut in pay in 1933 down 10 or 20 percent. Berger dropped from $10,000 to $9,000. The cuts, justified or not, were inflicted with the stated proposition that they would be made up for if attendance at Braves Field in 1933 was as good as 1932. It was not, but the Judge wrote Berger before the end of August: "I believe your spirit and the spirit of the club has done so much for Boston and the Braves that irrespective of whether or not [the 1932 level] is reached, I feel it is justly due you for me to reinstate the amount of your 1932 contract, and you will receive the proportionate amount of your cut in your salary check on the various pay days left this year. The first check to have the added share will be your salary check of September 1st.")

The record, even without recording-breaking salary figures, exhibits the Judge's attention to timing and to detail in bargaining. He appealed to Berger, successfully, invoking loyalty and praising Berger's "skill and hustle" while keeping a clear head. Berger got his raises regularly. Berger got raises when Braves shareholders were drawing no dividends whatever. Berger's pay cut was reinstated without regard to attendance figures and, typically, the Judge paid Berger a few hundred outside the contract as a voluntary "signing bonus." Berger never lost a sense of being underpaid by several thousands, never ceased to ask for more and to settle for less than he felt he deserved. In 1933, when everybody was taking cuts, he argued that he had expected a raise: "I will sign for the same salary as last year and consider that I have received a cut." Given Berger's mind-set, the Judge was a marvelous manager of men and negotiations. He not only brought "the new Babe Ruth" to Braves Field but kept him at Braves Field, productively, throughout the roughest years of the baseball business. But Berger was a player who worked out; other expensive players on the Braves roster did not. So far extended in risk was he, however, that when the hotly-touted and expensive players did not work out, and fans rebelled at the fall of their stars from the First Division and pennant-contending seasons just past, deserting Braves Field "in droves" (as Samuel Goldwyn would have put it) in 1934, the team was in the red and could not come up with the rent for Jim Gaffney's heirs. It was at this point that the Judge was most approachable that he received an invitation from New York, from Colonel Jacob Ruppert.

15

Colonel Ruppert's Invitation

"Years later when the old Yankees manager Joe McCarthy came to Boston and invited us out to eat, Joe asked the family if they knew why he thought so highly of the Judge. My sister Helen asked if it was because the Judge had taken Babe Ruth. Joe nodded and smiled, yes. We knew it was a complex situation. The full story will probably never be told. All of the participants died years ago. And Babe wasn't much of a writer."

— Bob Fuchs (1995)

"I told him Bill McKechnie was my friend and suggested that he didn't want to become a manager, that he'd be better off as an executive."

— Judge Fuchs, recalling advice
he gave Babe Ruth in 1935

There was between the Judge and Colonel Ruppert intense similarity and intense difference. Although both were cosmopolitan German-born sportsmen, acutely conscious of a code of honesty and gentlemanly deportment, his brewing empire and the Yankee dynasty stood behind Ruppert, elevating him to the "Hall of Fame" level of ownership, while the Judge stood darkly in the shadows of statistical deficit and low team achievements. Ruppert's call turned out to be The Call, a call to act, a call to salvation.

But Ruppert's motives in calling were certainly not unmixed. Although he, no doubt sincerely, wanted to help the Judge retain ownership of the Braves, he also had a white elephant on his hands. Ruppert, without money problems, had a unique problem. His problem was Babe Ruth. Ruppert had no place on his team for the aging athlete, not even — especially note —

in coaching or management. But Ruth had team and fan support. The Yankees, for example, were the only team without a team captain. Since Ruppert had suspended Ruth in 1925 nobody had stepped forward to fill the vacancy. Ruppert could not cross swords with Ruth and, in his present state of uncertain self-discipline, Ruth was unsaleable. But he stood in the way of Ruppert's ambitions for the Yankees to make of the thirties what they had of the twenties.

Ruppert wasted no conversation on his ambitions. He was courteous and deferential to the Judge, so recently and so publicly maligned. Ruppert made it clear that the Judge might be in a position to do him a great favor, if he would only take Ruth. Ruppert asked the Judge if he would consider signing Ruth on to the Braves. The Judge said something affirmative without making a commitment and, on the strength of that alone, Ruppert asked that he name a place and a time convenient to him. They would bring Ruth to him. The Judge named the Biltmore Hotel and designated a date and time. Colonel Ruppert and Yankees General Manager, Ed Barrows, escorted Ruth to the Judge's hotel room. The Yankees' owner knew his man. The Judge liked to take on long-shot comeback players.

Among other aging athletes who had made their way to Boston before Ruth were George Sisler, Johnny Evers and Rabbit Maranville. Casey Stengel had been dropped on the Braves by the Giants more than ten years earlier, his legs gone. Mostly, their bat had lost its smack and they got mileage off defensive playing skills within the huge field built for another era. There was always a place on the Braves for a player with good fielding, who could play with his head, trading off experience for deficits in speed or coordination. (The Judge even recruited players for comeback attempts himself. One of the most popular Boston players, 1914 Braves star Hank Gowdy — first player to enlist in World War I — served the Judge as coach for years. The Judge activated his veteran "patriot" to catch one Fourth of July. When Gowdy not only caught a good game but went four-for-four at the plate, the Judge insisted he stay on the lineup. As Gowdy ceased immediately batting a thousand and diminished his record by increments each appearance at bat in games thereafter, the Judge decommissioned him from further active service!)

The Judge's position in February 1935, was better by a bit than it had been in December. New England governors and mayors prodded by Governor Curley, had rallied behind a preseason ticket sales campaign that neatly paid the $40,000 owed from last season so that when the Judge met with the Yankee delegation the team he owned was technically in the black and could break even, especially if the new landlord, the National League itself, subsidized or extended the largest single cost besides payroll, the annual field rent. With President Roosevelt's son, insurance executive James Roosevelt, the Judge was exploring possibilities for bank loans in anticipation of the looming promissory note. Banks saved and reopened by the federal government owed a lot to the Roosevelt administration and something might yet gel to tide things over in the summer, with or without an explosion of team revenues. While still far at sea, the Judge hoped that the light he saw was not a gleam in his eye, but home port. But he needed something more to feel confident of making it. That is when Ruppert's call came, and the visit occurred at which Babe Ruth was offered him.

New York had galvanized him into action before 1935. After all, but for John McGraw, Christy Mathewson and a comment by George M. Cohan, the Judge would not have become owner of the Braves. Events in New York had led to the Braves' acquisition of Rogers Hornsby. When Colonel Ruppert thought about a Yankees team without Babe Ruth in February 1935, the Judge's help was naturally sought to provide the star with a "soft landing" as player-manager in a Boston Braves uniform.

The Judge, energized, did most of the talking with Ruppert after the subject was clear and, for once, he talked to get a good deal for himself. The premise of exchange was that the Judge would get a financial boost in helping Ruth to land a position with a team as a manager-in-training.

Having been a Judge presiding over a busy night court in New York City, by 1935 a former baseball manager and, for over ten years, the owner of a major league team, on friendly, if not first-name, terms with just about every baseball player of note, owner and baseball writer, the Judge was not speechless before Babe Ruth. Babe Ruth the man, after all, retained much of Babe Ruth the boy. Advice from others (ultimately, from his wife) often became the Babe's own plan of action. Colonel Ruppert was neither the first nor the last in the parade of authority figures who encouraged Babe Ruth with advice. Colonel Ruppert suggested that he try the Boston Braves. The Judge suggested that he wear three hats at first, inching into management as assistant to Bill McKechnie, while adding to team goodwill and revenues as itinerant vice-president doing public relations, without losing the opportunity to extend his playing days while racking up additional personal records in the game. It appealed to Ruth. Probably, he thought he could do everything. He was at home in the spotlight and enjoyed pleasing crowds far from the ballpark. Seclusion was a natural match for the Babe, sating his hunger for public acclaim while exercising his extroversion. To get into management through Bill McKechnie should be the equivalent of a one-student master's class. To play ball with the Braves would be a very big frog in a very small pond. Boston fans recalled him fondly. A sold-out Fenway Park had given him a standing ovation in 1934 at what he and the fans thought might be his last appearance at a game in Boston. Without losing his salary, bridging the gap between playing and retiring from playing, retaining Yankee good will at the same time, with some possibility of financial return on Braves stock (the team that had bumped up into First Division in 1933 and 1934), Babe faced 1935 with high hopes. Unless the Braves regressed or Boston fans abandoned their favorite team, Boston would be a good place for Babe Ruth to be mid–Depression. Only by hindsight was the deal a bad one. As a matter of marketing the skills he possessed, Babe Ruth's trade to Boston had the makings of a "good career move."

But the conversion was a discussion between New Yorkers. The Judge first meeting Ruth, went through his updated credentials, naming names to inspire Ruth not merely to join the Braves, but to join the New Yorkers who cared about one another and worked together, and who wanted to help the Judge stay in baseball. Staying in baseball would be these two New Yorkers' common denominator.

"Babe," he said, "I'm anxious to have you come back to Boston." He invited Ruth's attention to Boston as the city where he had excelled as a pitcher, where fans would welcome his arrival as a "return." But the Judge made explicit the New York scene as less inviting.

"I know it was your ambition to be considered as a candidate for manager of the Yankees when your playing days were over," he said with Colonel Ruppert and Ed Barrows seated beside them. "I know that Colonel Ruppert told you, when you complained first about Miller Huggins and later about Joe McCarthy, that he could not consider you as a manager until you learned how to manage yourself." The Judge, judging Ruth would have remembered that discussion but nonetheless retained his interest in managing, assured him of consideration on exactly the same basis.

"I am perfectly willing to make you an executive vice-president of the club where you will continue to be connected with the Braves when your playing days are over," the Judge said. It was as a team executive vice-president that Ruth was expected to make the lucrative appearances or tours from which team revenues would be enhanced, whether he played or not. His celebrity status entitled him to that enduring connection.

"As to your suggestion of assistant manager, I will be glad to announce that position with the understanding that the circumstances which compelled Colonel Ruppert to deny you the position of manager have changed," the Judge said, adding, "in which event I will not stand in your way if you can qualify as a big league manager."

This last statement led back to Colonel Ruppert emphatically claiming that Ruth could stake his place as manager with the Yankees on the basis of his work as the Braves' assistant manager. The Judge would not stand in his way. The same ladder he had climbed up from Boston to New York as a player was offered in big league management.

"I know you will understand," the Judge told Ruth. He was not offered the job of Braves manager, educating him if he did not understand, "that Bill McKechnie has given me faithful service and, as long as he desires to stay with me, no change will be made." But this comment did nothing to sour the deal that Ruth felt he was making with the Judge in a room with Colonel Ruppert and Ed Barrows: it was, after all, not the position of manager of the Braves that Ruth lusted for, but the same spot with the Yankees. What came far closer to nixing any deal was its final negotiation, over the manner in which Ruth could and would help the Judge in his financial distress. Neither Ruth (the best-paid player in history since 1920, who justified his 1930 salary's exceeding the president's on grounds that he'd "had a better year than Hoover") nor the Yankees nor Colonel Ruppert had had recent appreciation of financial distress. The Judge faced his hardest selling job beginning with a pitch inside and slow.

The Judge did not exaggerate. He faced a $200,000 loan with six months to pay during a deepening worldwide depression. His sole asset was a ball team that had finished fourth during its final game of the preceding season. One game in September 1934, at Braves Field against Brooklyn, was attended by only 400 fans. The team had gone from overfilling the place to playing to an empty house. When the Judge engaged Babe Ruth by contract on February 27, 1935, under which Ruth's salary would be $35,000, the Judge had only just paid the 1934 rent on Braves Field, through massive advance ticket sales. The contract was a last hurrah in the face of extinction. It had been years since Ruth could command such a salary and years since the Judge could pay it, but none of this mattered to either of them. Both looked for a second wind, a rebirth, a miracle at Braves Field in 1935. The Judge explained his need and hopes carefully to Ruth.

"I need your help more than you need me. The players on the Braves' roster have been very loyal to me. They go to smokers and dinners to create good will for the Braves."

This loyalty was reciprocal; the Judge knew Ruth was friendly with Rabbit Maranville and had probably already heard that he had offered Maranville the manager's job before he had managed the club for himself. In praising Maranville, the Judge also found a way to weave New York names into his argument with Ruth, whose life was now totally New York.

"Rabbit went everywhere if he could help the club," the Judge said. "At the sports writers dinner in New York he made a speech in which he expressed his affection for me, and at the same dinner my old friend Will Rogers spoke, and Mayor LaGuardia. The reason for their kind words was their concern that financial circumstances might compel me to get out of baseball."

With this much, the Judge asked Ruth to take part in exhibition games.

Ruth, while being indirectly reminded that big Braves stars speak at sports writers dinners in New York occasionally, and that the Braves owner was recognized fondly in New York as a friend of its most celebrated men, exhibited his own attention to business, asking a question in turn.

"Don't you think I ought to get a percentage of the exhibition games?" he asked.

Although this is likely not the first comment Ruth made, it is the first reported by the Judge in his description of that meeting. And it would have been a memorable slap in the face. It stayed in the Judge's memory for decades.

That was Ruth's question even after the Judge exposed his economic vulnerability and suggested by naming names that Ruth could corroborate that terrible situation. The Judge, seeking fiscal salvation, confessing his ownership of the Braves to be in jeopardy, having emphasized that he needed Ruth more than Ruth needed him, and offering loyalty for loyalty, was tossed back to a purely economic exchange.

The tension in the hotel room had reached its height. Ruth's question was the climax; the Judge's offer of a 25 percent share to Ruth was anti-climactic, as was the agreement for $35,000 a year to Ruth and no fee to the Yankees. The Judge attempted to recoup the possibility of a mutual loyalty at meeting's end, conjuring up the ghost of Christy Mathewson. But he prefaced his point with an acknowledgment that Ruth's present Yankee status was nonexistent.

"I don't think that I am violating any confidence when I say to you that I could not acquire your services if it weren't for the desire of Colonel Ruppert, Ed Barrows and Joe McCarthy to have you leave the Yankees and the house that Ruth Built — Yankee Stadium," the Judge said. "I will give you the same opportunity that I gave my old friend, Christy Mathewson. I don't want you to invest any money in the Braves, but I will set aside a substantial lot of stock so that if you bring the Braves up to a paying proposition, you will reap the benefit of it in addition to your salary and share of the exhibition games."

It was a needed *tour de force* by a masterful trial lawyer who had never lost a jury case. Much of his discussion with Ruth must have been prepared before he delivered it, much as an opening or closing statement may be prepared. The themes hit — and remembered expressly years afterward — were strong and appealing to Ruth's emotions. He intended that Ruth sign on with the Braves. If that meant stripping Ruth of any last illusion that he had the least power over "The House that Ruth Built" in 1935, it meant saying so, truthfully, clearly, with people listening and not correcting him.

But the discussion bore bitter fruit. New York was the carrot and New York was the stick at the same time. New York does not want you, so come to Boston. You can work out in Boston so that New York will want you. Ruth's thoughts remained on New York. His commitment — probably something he expected only to last one season — was half-hearted. He made no effort to develop relationships with other Braves or to crack Boston's social scene. He was in Boston only to get out of Boston as soon as he got the call. The Judge's hopes were different: for Ruth to make money while gradually disciplining himself and the Braves into a state of grace which would beckon Yankee attention at which point Ruth, part owner of the team, might decide to stay with the Braves.

The Judge and the Boston Braves were in no position to acquire Babe Ruth in February 1935 — but here he was. The Judge did not consult with his manager, Bill McKechnie. The decision was the Judge's to make and given the immediate alternative of a mortgage to pay and the persistent reality of a Braves deficit, it was a decision with only one answer: an opportunity to save Babe Ruth for baseball while he saved the Braves for the Judge.

Failure seemed so likely that even the Judge's partner, Charles Francis Adams, held nothing back publicly in welcoming Babe Ruth to the team, and to reality. Adams' sober greeting at the banquet was chilly and prophetic:

"Bill McKechnie was frank, honest and correct when he said there can be but one boss," Adams said, underlining by repetition a remark of the manager whom Ruth longed to replace but whom Adams termed his "personal representative." Given Adams' partnership holdings and status as creditor, the warning was a strong one; Adams went on, talking in the third person of the baseball hero in the hotel dining room before him and all assembled celebrities.

He said that the Babe had much to learn. "He must learn to be a good soldier," Adams declared, capping that with an ambiguous jibe, "if he is not one already. He must by his own example create loyalty and respect within and without the club."

Adams was asking Babe Ruth to step down from his pedestal, to become obedient at age 40, enlisting in the Braves army as a "good soldier."

16

Babe Ruth: The Second Coming

"Babe called everybody 'Stud.' If he introduced anybody, he'd say, 'Stud, I want you to meet Stud.' He never knew anybody's name."
— Elbie Fletcher on Babe Ruth

Babe Ruth and his wife joined the Judge on the midday train from New Haven to Boston. The Judge reported the triumph, which snowballed as the train got closer to the Hub:

> Crowds gathered at the New Haven station, then a larger one at the Providence station, where Boston's sports writers got aboard with us. Besides newspaper reporters, there was a crew from a Boston radio station. Once we got within range of the city, they had the Babe speak to the fans. It was said to be the first time a broadcast had been made from a moving train.
>
> Thousands were at the Back Bay station to welcome him back to Boston. The mayor, Fred Mansfield, a friend of mine and a great Braves fan, was on hand with local celebrities and prominent citizens. The day ended with a huge banquet in the Babe's honor at the Copley Plaza.

Apart from the Judge's partner, Charles Francis Adams, nobody reminded the Babe to behave. At the time, such advice seemed unnecessary. The Babe performed well during spring training. For the first time in the Judge's tenure, the team's exhibition games in St. Petersburg were sold out. Ruth was in fine condition as an athlete.

Austen Lake captured the mood during a dinner at St. Petersburg: "The Judge tapped a water glass with a coffee spoon and extolled the Babe's virtues until one doubted that this paragon of perfection could be the big sun-toasted mischief-maker whose midnight pranks and hilarious capers were a smoke house legend.

"And, in his turn, the Babe responded by blurting equal extravagances back at the Judge, sweetheart language which the Babe bounced off the walls in his booming basso."

The honeymoon continued on opening day; the Judge recalled: "On his first appearance at Braves Field he seemed to fulfill our fondest hopes by hitting a home run off Carl Hubbell and winning the game for Boston against the Giants. Mayor Mansfield, occupying the box with me, turned to me as the ball went over the fence and said, 'Judge, your problems are over!' So it seemed."

The 1935 season (which was actually Wally Berger's best season) began auspiciously enough. The Braves took on the Giants in Boston on April 16, then the Giants took on the Braves April 18 in New York. The Polo Grounds were packed, standing room only: over 47,000 that day constituted the largest opening day attendance in either league that year.

It had become obvious that the old war-horse, Rabbit Maranville, was not going to resume his place in the lineup. On May 22, 1935, he was given a testimonial dinner in Pittsburgh. Not only did the Judge sing praises of his former star but Babe Ruth, with tears, lamented the plight of a fallen star. The situation struck close to home. After a rejected attempt to retire on May 12, 1935, the Babe stayed on to hit three homers on May 25, 1935: number 714, his last, hit so hard by the left-handed powerhouse that it soared some 600 feet, clearing the right-field rooftop, something beyond any player's power before that.

The Judge was calculating and gambling on a good year with Ruth. The Braves had cleared a $150,000 profit in 1933 but that was last year's snowfall. In 1934 the top-heavy salaries of a barely First Division team caused a $40,000 deficit. The National League's guarantee of the Braves Field lease together with advance ticket sales provided only a break-even beginning or basis for hope. It was necessary to draw 1933-size crowds to the ball games and, primarily, to Braves Field, where the cut favored the home team so significantly. Filling the Polo Grounds provided the Braves with only 25 percent of the gate. But filling Braves Field provided three times that percentage. The Braves had to make it at home or not at all, and an empty park at Braves Field would be the end of the Judge as owner.

But the Judge's problems had actually increased. The Babe presented a problem in management. So used to adulation, he rode on trains in the owner's drawing room rather than in the coach with his fellow players. In his triple role as player–second vice president–assistant manager he was

Judge Fuchs day presentation is made by James M. Curley, governor of Massachusetts on April 16, 1935 (courtesy of the Boston Public Library, Print Department).

neither fish nor fowl. Politicians and sports writers crowded into the drawing room to be with, listen to and shake the hand of a baseball legend. The
team of old Braves, whose hopes had been raised to pennant-level only a
couple of seasons earlier, disappointed at falling back to second division
status, took the situation poorly. They resented a fading star's aloofness.
They found it aggravating that one whose salary had led every other player
in baseball, a rich man, should command a percentage of exhibition games
of 25 percent. (And their ire was greater if they ever learned that the Babe
was the only player ever to collect simultaneously a percentage of exhibition games from two teams. In 1935 he retained moneys from Yankees exhibition games while receiving the quarter-share promised of Braves exhibition games.)

   Babe Ruth was like an injection into a patient. Side reactions were
kicking off which threatened the life of the victim. The Judge brought the
Babe and McKechnie together for a meeting soon after the season began.
He pled with both, seeking their help and cooperation.

   The idea was that Ruth the player would go a few innings a game and
not play in every game, conserving his diminishing powers, but being available as needed in close games to make a difference. Ruth the assistant man-

ager would pep up the team spirit and give his fellow batsmen some pointers in the art of hitting. Ruth the second vice-president would build up the team's financial base and goodwill via personal appearances and autograph signing. If it worked, the Babe and the Judge would be able to stay in baseball actively.

It did not work out as hoped.

Ruth was virtually played out; his homer off Hubbell masked a serious deficit in skills.

Wally Berger, "Boston's Babe Ruth," literally stepped aside for the Bambino. Berger had been number 3 in the Braves uniform for several seasons. In deference to the star, who wanted to wear it, Berger dropped down a peg to be number 4. The reactions of neither player is recorded. But his number switch was not the only accommodation players were asked to make. The Babe — whose interest in managing, especially managing his old team, the Yankees, burned within him — was a player-executive with emphasis on the executive, in his mind. Players resented it, emphasizing in their minds that he was the best-paid player on the team but not otherwise the team's best player. Although he made no judgment errors on the

Legendary slugger Babe Ruth, who ended his playing days with the Boston Braves in 1935, signs an autograph for a sports writer as Judge Fuchs (second from left) looks on (reprinted with permission of the *Boston Herald*).

Joe Cronin, Babe Ruth and Bill McKechnie in 1935 (courtesy of the Boston Public Library, Print Department).

field, he was slowing down. Years of no discipline had gotten to him physically. He was overweight and his legs were giving out on him.

The Babe's rugged attention to himself during spring training took pounds off, but could not reverse years of squandered resources.

His wife knew it and was unafraid to admit it.

When newspaper reporters asked her about her attendance at all of the Braves' games, she was quick to define her interest.

"No, I am not at the game because I am a fan," she said. She drove the Babe to and from the game because, on the way, "the Babe needs every bit of energy" and after a game "he needs to relax."

The Ruths' joint efforts to conserve the aging star's energies worked in spurts. His performance was erratic enough, however, that fans ceased to buy tickets on the basis of seeing the Babe hit a homer.

Ruth the assistant manager was a title without meaning. Ruth maintained distance and established no bonds between himself and the up-and-coming players. They were foreign to him. The Braves and Boston were not and could never be the Yankees and New York. He was homesick and it affected his coaching motivation.

Ruth the vice-president enjoyed the most success. However, he broke with the Judge over public appearances. He asserted a claim of ownership. It was his question, whether he ought to get a percentage of exhibition games, grown into questions of percentages of ticket sales. Ticket sales were typically behind the speeches or autograph days arranged for the Babe. That is, Jordan Marsh or some other business would purchase blocks of tickets to give away or to use as promotions because the Braves promised an appearance by the Babe on-site.

The Judge actively enlisted fellow Boston businessmen in the army supporting his ownership of the Braves. Although the Judge recalled the businessmen calling him, rather than his calling them, the Judge probably had some idea of the commercial possibilities of Babe Ruth's public appearances; the need for such deals was in the Judge rather than in other Boston businesses; and the Judge felt (rightly) confident of the Babe's cooperation. When a newspaper publisher and the head of the Jordan Marsh department store offered to buy a block of seats at Braves Field if the Babe would address a group of young boys at the Boston Arena and do some autographing, the Judge secured Babe's cooperation. After a few days, the Babe came to speak with the Judge. His wife thought he ought to get $2,000 to speak. The Judge could hardly believe it. The thought outraged his sense of honor, as he had accepted the engagement. Not only was a man's word his bond, youngsters would be disappointed. After a reminder that the team's vice president was to help establish team goodwill, the Babe — who apparently had only relayed a suggestion by his wife — agreed to go through with the appearance as scheduled, and later did so.

But this agreement was reached only after he threatened not to do them — perhaps not to do any more, ever — because he wanted to go to New York.

The Babe wanted to capitalize on his success. Three horses were dragging him toward New York at once: his desire to be adored by the New York fans (including many celebrities in their own right), his homesickness, and an ability to schedule himself. The Judge's insistence on the point was galling. The Judge drew a line around Ruth to remind him that he was working for a team that needed him in Boston while simultaneously reserving or preserving Ruth's public appearances as a sort of Braves asset or monopoly. There was nothing in the Judge's refusal to permit Ruth to go to New York that was inconsistent with his earliest arrangement with Ruth: the team's revenue needs, the Babe's own liabilities as player and manager, Ruth's discipline of himself. Babe, eating, drinking and back in New York presented problems for the Judge. Their deal was in jeopardy by his attitude of facing

New York instead of Boston, looking to New York rather than Boston for emotional succor and, ultimately, public appearances or money.

Ultimately, it was not New York but an ocean liner headed for New York from France which led to the confrontation which led Babe Ruth to hang up his Braves uniform on June 2, 1935.

17

Babe Ruth: The Second Leaving

"Ruth would have been the manager some day if he had been a good soldier, and hadn't asked for extra privileges."
— Judge Fuchs, on Babe Ruth's departure (1935)

New York's elite were to meet to eat aboard the *Normandie* when she docked in New York Harbor on arrival from her maiden voyage.

On Thursday, May 30, 1935, two clocks began to tick.

One was the *Normandie*, beginning what would be a record-breaking crossing of the Atlantic. Its state-of-the-art engines shot the world's largest ocean liner (the first to exceed 1,000 feet from bow to stern) from Europe to America in style. The *Normandie* was not just another ship at sea; it was the world's largest turbo-electric generator, period. Nothing on sea or land equaled its power (160,000 sea-horsepower). Built to carry 2,000 people across the Atlantic in comfort and safety, the Blue Riband–winning vessel shot across the sea in four days, three hours and two minutes. No people had ever bridged the gap between Europe and America in a shorter time over water. Big news in 1935, the *Normandie* was France's answer to the Depression and the future of transatlantic travel. For it to arrive on time was important. For 10,000 people to pay for the fifty-cent tour of the ship the day it arrived was great. But for its true christening as a celebrated vessel, celebrities were needed and invited from every walk of life. The people sending out invitations for the gala party presided over by the wife of the President of France hoped to score a hit with Babe and Mrs. Ruth. They were, along with 700 others, invited to dine on the *Normandie* the evening of Tuesday, June 4, 1935.

The other clock was biological. Time was running out for the Babe's active career as player. Immediately upon the team's return to Boston from its western road trip, Bill McKechnie sought out the Judge. On Thursday, May 30, McKechnie told the Judge that Ruth could not go on.

A couple of weeks earlier, after a poor showing in a Sunday game against the Cubs on May 12, Ruth himself had broached the subject of leaving. But the Judge thought that Ruth should take time to shake off a bad cold he had and then, rather than leave when he was not doing well, leave at the top of his game. Not only had Ruth heeded the advice, but the opportunity foretold by the Judge came true almost magically at Forbes Field in Pittsburgh where, in a single game, in a place previously without any outside-the-park home runs, on May 25, 1935, Ruth slugged away like the champion he had been, or even better, with three over-the-fence jobs. (His last three-homers-in-one-game day had been in 1926.)

McKechnie, however, was more than concerned about risk of injury; he faced a pitchers' mutiny. There were threats by some not to take the mound with Ruth in right field. Riding the crest of a wave now breaking, Ruth had not retired. But his body had. His legs were going out from under him. He could still hit. And he could hobble. But he could not run.

That Thursday as the Judge listened to McKechnie he temporized. He insisted that McKechnie have Cantwell, Frankhouse and Betts put their complaints in writing, signed, before he would act or confront Ruth.

But the Judge needed no tactic of his own to buy time. The Babe had turned himself over to a doctor for an examination of his legs. The doctor concluded that there was a risk of "water on the knee." Several days' rest were in order. Several days, that is, including Tuesday and Wednesday. The invitation burned a hole in his pocket. It made no sense to stay in Boston to sit on the bench in sparsely-attended Braves Field with his indifferent teammates when he could be taking part in the best party in the country, a celebrity among celebrities.

The Babe presented both the doctor's orders and his invitation. He thought it would be a good thing for baseball if he attended, he told the Judge. He had been invited, he was sure, as representative of baseball. In this respect, he was probably quite correct. The same aspect which had, that past winter, presented Colonel Ruppert with a problem, and which had attracted a crowd on Broadway much as a magnet attracts iron filings when he had walked with the Judge to the brewery, now in late spring stood clearly behind his invitation from the French government: Babe Ruth represented baseball. Commission Landis's door might claim that aspect as his in Chicago, but the voice of the people hailed the Babe. And forty million

Frenchmen could hardly be wrong in seeing in the aging player all that he had been and what baseball could be at its best. The Babe wanted to go to New York, but New York was coming to Boston.

The *Normandie* party would have to take place without him. The good of baseball that he aspired to serve, the Judge responded, required his attendance at Braves Field. Special trains were bringing hundreds of fans of all ages to see Brooklyn take on Boston because they wanted to see the Babe. And even if he only stood to take a bow, he owed it to his fans to appear. There had been publicity. The Babe was expected. The Judge felt it was a public promise.

For the Judge the decision had been simple. Given doctor's orders excusing the Babe from taking left field, there would be no mutiny on the mound for at least the next several days. But the team and its owner both needed every bit of mileage they could possibly receive from Babe Ruth as an icon of American baseball. Balanced against that concrete need, time off to attend a glitzy party on a luxury liner seemed a frivolous waste of baseball's "ambassador."

The Babe mulled things over, understanding the Judge's answer to be final.

The *Normandie* was halfway across the Atlantic on Sunday, June 2, 1935. Babe Ruth called for the gentlemen of the press to hear an announcement: he was all done with the Braves. As the *Normandie's* record-breaking days were just beginning, Babe Ruth was hanging up his last major league uniform, gray with blue stripes and a red-fringed "B."

Babe Ruth's second leaving of Boston was, as in 1920, to New York. However, in 1920 he had been sold by Harry Frazee to finance a Broadway musical, the hit show *No, No, Nanette*. In 1935 he left for his own reasons, to take part in another part of New York nightlife. A reporter who visited the Ruths as they packed in the hotel room before taking the train out of South Station for New York on Monday recalled he was tearless over his departure.

"Hell, kid, we all strike out sometime," he told Austen Lake of the *Boston-American*. He told other reporters that he was looking for something else in baseball.

He never found it.

And the Judge, having lost Babe Ruth, lost his Boston Braves.

18

Fair Ball

"If we want a first division club, we've got to pay major league salaries."
— Christy Mathewson (1923)

In reprise, what Christy Mathewson said had to happen did happen, though not in his lifetime. "Big Six" had been over three years dead when, in 1929, the Braves began to change. The same year the stock market crashed, the same season the Judge managed the team himself (to a slightly better win-loss record than the 1928 Hornsby year), Boston found the Braves. On the strength of home-game receipts, the Braves began to show a profit. It was in Braves Field and not on circuit in the National League that the Braves raised the moneys to pay the salaries to attract the players that would put the team up into the First Division, not only in 1933 but also in 1934. Boston fans made it happen. Other cities remained cold to the Braves; the team's "away" game revenue stagnated at $100,000 year after year. But the turnstiles at Braves Field churned. The sum of $200,000 gross during the Hornsby year shot up and almost doubled at $350,000 in 1929, while the Judge managed much the same players to almost the same record but colorfully.

Finding good players is an art and not a science. The Judge told stories against himself, like the time John McGraw wanted Braves pitcher Larry Benton. McGraw offered Bill Terry. The Judge insisted instead on first baseman "Long John" Kelley. Terry's great bat went elsewhere. Later, when Rogers Hornsby was managing in 1928, the Judge declined Hornsby's advice that the Braves claim Joe Cronin. "He can't hit," the Judge told Hornsby. A player the Judge quite rightly thought could hit the first time he saw him was Hank Greenberg. When the Judge saw Greenberg at the plate in Tampa, he was flush with cash and confidence. He immediately made the Detroit owner Frank Nevin an offer he could not–but did–refuse of $75,000. (Ironically, Nevins later offered waivers on Greenberg for $7,500 and, that failing, sent him to the minors for a season; but Greenberg's comeback is baseball legend.) Although the Judge wrote that the two most attractive features of baseball were "color and base stealing," in which John McGraw's ideal is mirrored, he only seemed to have eyes for hitters and to assess players favorably or unfavorably by focusing on their batting skills, the kind of game preferred by Colonel Ruppert's Yankees. It was, finally, natural that the Judge would accept the services of Babe Ruth. It was only appropriate that the long-standing record for lifetime home runs would be made by a player for Judge Fuchs's Boston Braves. It was only natural that one of his Braves, Wally Berger, would set the rookie record for homers, Braves Field notwithstanding. Babe Ruth, whose bat had checked John McGraw, was finally removed from "the game of yards" and placed in "the game of inches."

People turned out to see the action. They were drawn, as true believers, to fair ball. Home interest grew even as the Depression deepened and attendance at ball parks nationwide steeply declined. Bostonians paid $450,000 hard-earned Depression dollars to see games at Braves Field in 1930. Other sports promoters in Boston were attracted. Hoping that the spectacle of a heavyweight fight would keep the crowds from leaving following the afternoon Braves games, boxing promoters of the Boston Garden paid $25,000 to lease Braves Field for boxing matches at night. But it was the Braves the people had come to see. The fights did not draw them to stay and the Boston Garden officials negotiated a buyback of the lease, to cancel it. Fans willing to do without supper to see the Boston Braves did not do so to see a fight.

The Judge had a rule never to sell a player. "No club can sell a player," he told a reporter once. "It has to get players in return."

He was proud of his record in terms of dollars; measured by dollars spent buying trades against dollars paid him for trades, he actually paid out more than he took in over years of trading some player or players for other players. The math demonstrated a commitment to the team, a personal proof of his being in the game for its greatness rather than for the gain.

With "new blood" in 1929 as a result of the lopsidedly favorable deal with the Chicago Cubs for Rogers Hornsby, and additional talent such as Wally Berger, with a cluster of winning pitchers in the thirties, the Boston Braves drew its largest crowds.

Auto tycoon Henry Ford attended a Braves and Tigers exhibition game in 1933. He had made up his mind to buy the up-and-coming Braves, a judgment concurred in by the then–Tigers president, Frank Navin.

The game went 14 innings. First baseman for the Braves, Baxter Jordan, began to argue with the umpire. The umpire had ruled a runner safe; Jordan thought he had tagged the man for a final out. During the argument Heinie Manush, an alert Tiger on third, stole home. The game was over. The Braves lost.

Although the Judge so loved a good story that he spun out the yarn of the loss of this particular exhibition game as if it made Henry Ford change his mind about buying the Braves, it was not so: the Judge himself refused to negotiate with Ford, as he later declined interest from Joseph Kennedy. His team was at the threshold and crossing over into the First Division, with pennant territory straight ahead and possibly, finally, a World Series. It was that story — a happy ending — that motivated the Judge.

Joseph Kennedy, moving money around in Hollywood, stocks and banks, came to present the Judge with an offer in the early thirties. With the sportsman and longtime editor of the New York *World*, Herbert Bayard Swope, Kennedy offered $600,000. The Judge characteristically regretted not having accepted because he felt that Kennedy and Swope "would have been great assets to baseball" rather than because he missed an opportunity to recoup his fortune.

The Braves of the thirties were lucky. Their hitting got better at a time other clubs' hitting got worse. Using Babe Ruth as a benchmark, the Babe was the last player to hit over .400 and he did that in the 1930 season. For a team to be gifted with a golden bat at any time is fine, but to have even a brass bat when others turn to iron makes for a good year. The 1931–35 environment allowed the Braves' improvement to make a startling difference in the team's competitiveness. They won more games. They looked better. They ran a close second for the pennant for a while. They finished in the First Division not once but two seasons in a row. They made use of a window of opportunity. The 1933 and 1934 seasons were unforgettable.

First Division had precise meaning. It translated easily into "pennant contender." It foreshadowed a championship. Indeed, the history of the Braves demonstrates the point quite neatly. They were "bottom feeders" for years until George Stallings whipped them up into a First Division team, finishing the 1913 season in fifth place. That achievement turned into a World Series sweep in four games in 1914. Fourth or fifth place most seasons meant a tidy profit: fourth place literally a share in World Series profits, fifth place vouching for a team's credibility. This goal eluded the Judge throughout the twenties but buoyed him and his team up almost as

soon as Depression struck the rest of the country and the sport of baseball.

During the 1934-35 winter, after an idea for nighttime greyhound racing at Braves Field failed to win approval, the Judge linked up with Governor Curley and Democratic mayors of Massachusetts. The politicians' *ad
hoc* committee sold season tickets to pay off the $40,000 rent arrears. The
Judge then secured from the National League a guarantee on the lease of
Braves Field. Opening day at the Wigwam was saved.

Running hard to keep pace with the Depression, the Judge reached out
to accept Colonel Ruppert's Babe Ruth, with all his strengths and weak-
nesses. The Judge was hopeful; with two consecutive First Division seasons
under his belt, he was entitled to some optimism. But baseball was changing, too.

The business edge of baseball was sharpening. On Sunday, April 29,
1934, Pittsburgh, the country's last holdout, offered major league baseball
on Sundays, too. On May 24, 1935, Franklin D. Roosevelt threw a switch
and there was light — the country's first night baseball game. It was now
baseball seven days a week, day and night. In this increasingly competitive
world, fighting over fewer fan dollars, the Judge was something of an
anachronism. In spite of the spreading Depression the Judge bet more than
his last dollar on everything working in 1935, the year everything unrav-
eled instead and the team sank to the bottom of the league (and benchmark of bad records).

The Judge was in no position to recover from investments that did not
pay off. Taking risks on talented players who did not work out was a luxury of the twenties, a way to play the game when there had been a margin
and he had had an active and lucrative New York law practice. That era of
playing for fun had ended in 1929. Beginning in 1929, with success for several years, the Judge played in earnest. But in 1935 it ended. Some so wished
the Boston Braves away that they changed the name of the team (to the
"Boston Bees," briefly, beginning in 1936). The movement to erase the name
was unsuccessful; they resumed the name and they carried it with them
when they moved first to Milwaukee and then to Atlanta. And the history
of the Boston Braves could not be erased any more successfully.

The Braves had been named after New Yorkers who had asserted themselves to be members of the "Tammany Tribe," inheriting their character
from their colorful New York owner, James Gaffney. The Braves remained
the Braves under successor sachems through their last New York owner,
Judge Fuchs. Chief of the "Tribe" headquartered at the "Braves Wigwam"
from 1923 to 1935, the Judge had shut down his law office and moved

himself and his family from New York to Boston. He never returned to live in New York. Governor Curley appointed the Judge first chairman of the Massachusetts Unemployment Commission upon his loss of his Braves ownership. The Judge went on to open a law office at 11 Beacon Street in Boston, across the street from the courts, a place where as much time was spent meeting old friends, baseball fans and sports writers as meeting clients.

In this connection, the words of the Judge's friend, Al Smith, rang true. Smith had written years earlier:

> My Dear Emil,
>
> As a boyhood friend, I was delighted to see that you are back in control of the Boston Braves. I was pleased to see that one who had devoted his life and money in the interest of friendship and good deeds, found friends in Boston, who, in a dozen years, were able to appreciate what we, your old friends, have known for a lifetime.
>
> All good wishes to you,
> Alfred E. Smith

In Boston, Governor Curley's help was of varied utility. Governor Curley was besieged by inventors who sought his help in promoting their inventions. Curley would send them to the Judge.

U.S. Marshall Murphy came up with a machine with which one could write in the sky. The Judge went up to Canada with Murphy and the inventor and the first night the test was positive. That night the test was made on a mountain and the clouds were low. The second night the sky was clear with no clouds and the writing in the sky no longer worked!

Then there were the rubber horseshoes, designed to replace the iron shoes on race horses with a lighter substitute. At first the group had to find a glue which would adhere and when they found a powerful glue which did adhere, it was so powerful that once on, they couldn't get it off. End of that venture!

There was also an attractive cane topped by a light, to be used for reading programs at the opera and theater. Too few cane-sporting men about town attended the opera during the Depression to market the device.

A man who contended that he held the deed to property in South America—and had evidence in the form of a transcript of his appearance before Congress advocating that his land be used to build a second Panama Canal—wanted the Judge's help. A South American title investigation revealed the businessman's title to the property had long been invalidated, and foreclosed for nonpayment of taxes.

Clients such as these aside, the new Judge continued to attend ball games of the Braves and Red Sox. His New York, the New York of Jimmy Walker, speakeasies, Damon Runyon and Ring Lardner, was gone. But his "second home" remained — baseball. It was baseball over anything else every time there was a question of priorities; the best example of this was his response to requests that he write his memoirs. He had intimate recollections of famous politicians in victory and defeat, exciting election stories and anecdotes of the leaders of this century, including Theodore Roosevelt, Franklin Roosevelt, Al Smith, Herbert Hoover, Charles Evans Hughes and many, many others.

The Judge had the "inside story" of some of his time's most famous political and legal events. But in response to his family's repeated requests that he write his memoirs, he wrote only a few pages on politics. He wrote over a hundred pages on baseball and the Boston Braves. The Judge had worked with and known well many famous people, but when he came to write he thought of such things and people as the Braves' pitcher Eddie Brandt's dilemma. Had it been otherwise, this book could not have been

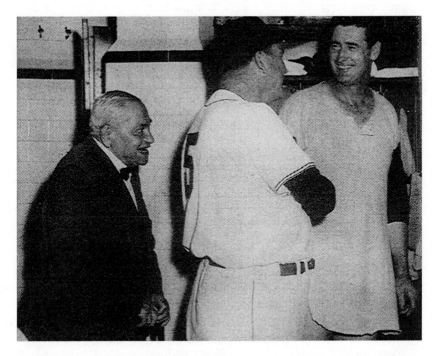

Judge Emil Fuchs and Manager Mike Higgins congratulate Ted Williams in the Red Sox clubhouse after "The Splendid Splinter" homered in his final major league at-bat in 1960 (reprinted with permission of the *Boston Herald*).

written — nor ought it to have been written. After all, a book about a man who owns a team as a possession is a book of no value. A book about a man who possessed an ideal which he attempted to serve to his best ability, who tried hard and basically succeeded — to the money-backed appreciation and recognition of Boston fans beginning in 1929, and to the record books with player and team performance — is a book that is justified.

The Judge's character, so wrong for the business of baseball, so right for its sport and its fun, suited him for ownership in the world of the Boston Braves of the twenties and thirties. And it was, thus, an earned earthly reward and blessing that the Judge was able to, and did, mentally relive those heady days, those adventures, those times of happiness and of sadness, days of hopes and frustrations, the years of his ownership of the Boston Braves, all years of fair ball.

Owners of major league baseball teams (which may now mean a bank or a purely business partnership) need to know when to buy and when to sell. For the Judge, who derived his knowledge of when to buy from one of the most perceptive team buyers in history, John McGraw, there was also a New York scene when it came to selling. In his memoirs, as part of a longer explanation of his retention of a game-losing, money-losing team, he reported something he had heard from Jim Gaffney, who had seen his Braves win the World Series in 1914, who had given the team that name and who had built Braves Field.

> Before he purchased the Boston club, Gaffney had come close to buying Brooklyn. The negotiations had been practically completed. Charley Ebbets had decided to sell. This was before the club played its games on what is now Ebbets Field.
> "As I recall it," Mr. Gaffney said, "the asking price was a little less than $300,000. I handed a certified check to Mr. Ebbets for the agreed amount. He took it into his hand and looked at it."
> Tears came into his eyes and he said, "Jim, I can't leave the old game. It has been my life. I would not know what to do with myself if I were out of baseball. Here, Jim, take this check back before I change my mind."

The Judge never put his hand out for such a check or followed through on offers made. But, like Charley Ebbets, he reached a stage in which baseball was his life and he could not leave the "old game." Even after losing the Braves, he remained in baseball as a fan and erstwhile (war-time) sports writer in Boston. "He never missed a game" is said of many fans with less justification. The Judge attended Braves and Red Sox games, rarely missing any. He enjoyed being close to the action. Newsreels taken at the time Ted Williams hit a 415-foot homer to cap his career depict him leaving home plate to shake hands: the first hand he shook was the Judge's. The image of the fan — the Judge as fan — is indelibly preserved in a newsreel of that day duplicated and used in Ken Burns's *Baseball* documentary. Rightly, the Judge is in that film not as a lawyer or owner or manager but as a fan, reaching out to congratulate the achiever of baseball excellence. This picture is indeed worth a thousand words.

Epilogue
by Robert S. Fuchs

Sixty years have passed since the Judge last presided over the "Wigwam" and over forty years have passed since the "Tribe" moved away from Boston. However, neither the Judge nor his team has been forgotten in Boston.

The Boston Chapter of the Baseball Writers' Association of America annually commemorates one whom the Judge would have called "a player who kept the game honest and great" by electing a player "for long and meritorious service to baseball" to receive the Judge Emil Fuchs Award. This gracious manner of perpetuating his memory — begun in 1959, within his lifetime — tickled the Judge more than anything. The "scribes" were his associates during his Boston Braves years and after 1935 as well. His secretary Eddie Cunningham was elected by the reporters to serve in that capacity much as they had elected Braves manager Bill McKechnie.

The Boston Braves are fondly recalled as well. There is an active Boston Braves Historical Association, a chapter of the Society for American Baseball Research, which is 600 members strong. George Altison of Marlborough, Massachusetts, devotes countless hours to running that organization, including an annual meeting that serves also as a reunion of the old "Knot Hole Gang" and Braves players. Bob Brady of Braintree, Massachusetts, publishes a fact-filled newsletter for members. I never read a copy without learning something new and amazing about the Boston Braves. The Association recently honored the memory of Judge Fuchs by electing him to its "Hall of Fame." Nothing would have pleased him more.

The plaque reads:

Hall of Famer Ernie Banks accepts the first Judge Emil Fuchs Memorial Award in 1959 from Judge Fuchs (left) and Eddie Cunningham, former secretary of the Boston Braves.

JUDGE EMIL E. FUCHS

BOSTON BRAVES

1923–1935
OWNER 1923–1935
MANAGER 1929

A true baseball fan who realized his dream to become a club owner, Judge Fuchs devoted his life and much of his personal wealth toward the betterment of Boston's National League franchise. During his reign the Judge brought Sunday baseball and radio broadcasting of games to Boston, established the Knot Hole Gang, sponsored frequent Ladies' Days at the "Wigwam" and returned Babe Ruth to the Hub. His 1933 team contended for the pennant until the last month of the season and set a club attendance record that endured until 1946. Among the many baseball notables that donned Braves flannels during the Fuchs era were Billy Southworth, Hank Gowdy, Rube Marquard, Casey Stengel, Dave Bancroft, Stuffy McInnis, Shanty Hogan, Johnny Cooney, George Sisler, Rogers Hornsby, Rabbit Maranville, Johnny Evers, Wally Berger, Burleigh Grimes and Bill McKechnie. Judge Fuchs passed away on December 5, 1961, but his contribution to Boston baseball has been memorialized by the Boston Baseball

Writers' Association's Judge Emil Fuchs Memorial Award for Long and Meritorious Service to Baseball."

When the Judge died Boston newspapers printed many tributes. Among them I have always treasured a poignant note by one who knew the Judge well, Hy Hurwitz of the *Globe*. After describing the Judge as devoted to the Braves, and acknowledging that Boston's baseball writers remembered the Judge's many kindnesses, Hurwitz concluded with the words that ought to end this book, as they ring true or, as my father sometimes put it, "they hit the ball right on the trademark":

"Baseball was his life."

Appendix A

In January, 1929, Judge Fuchs had to defend himself. His veracity was challenged during the Boston Finance Commission's investigation into the so-called "Sunday Baseball Scandal."

It was always up to a defendant to risk his reputation. Nobody can force it; the issue of one's reputation for truth and veracity is not injected but only volunteered. The Judge decided to bring the issue up; having lived almost his life in New York, his witnesses were almost all New Yorkers. Telegrams and statements were read into the record by Charles Francis Adams on January 22, 1929. As reported in the next day's *Traveler*,

> Those coming forward to the defense of Judge Fuchs included:
> Former Gov. Alfred E. Smith of New York.
> Mayor James J. Walker of New York.
> Charles M. Schwab, noted financier.
> Former Gov. Horace White.
> James R. Sheffield, former ambassador to Mexico.
> United States Senator Robert Wagner.
> Herbert Bayard Swope, ex-editor *New York World*.
> Jaob B. Banton, district attorney, New York county.
> Edward Schoenick, former Lieutenant-Governor of New York. Richard E. Enright, former police commissioner of New York.
> William Hayward, former United States district attorney.
> Leroy Scott, president of Authors' Society of America. Emory B. Buyckner, former United States district attorney.
> Charles D. Hilles, former secretary to President Taft and national committeeman of New York state.
> Charles B. Stover, oldest settlement worker in America and former fire commission.
> John A. Heydler, president of the National League. William H. Calder, former United States senator.
> William Collier, author and head of Writers' Club.
> Dr. Henry Moskowitz, president of American Art and former assistant to Dr. Felix Adler, Ethical Culture Society.

Prof. Frank H. Sommer, dean of New York University law school.
Chief Justice William G. McAdoo.
Meyer Bloomfield, former professor at Harvard and settlement worker.
Fr. Francis P. Duffy.
Mgr. Corry of Holy Name Church, New York city. Col.
Robert Guggenheim of Guggenheim Foundation.

FROM JUSTICES

Justices of the superior court of the state of New York and of the board of general sessions: Justice Otto A. Rosalsky, Justice Charles C. Nott, Jr., Justice Cornelius F. Collins, Justice Joseph Mulqueen, Justice Maurice Koenig, Justice Isodore Waservogel, Justice George Vincent Mullin, Justice Joseph E. Corrigan.

Robert Adamson, vice president of the bank of the United States and ex-fire commissioner of New York.

James McDonough, vice president of Manufacturers Trust Company.

Charles E. Heydt, vice president of Broadway Central Bank, election commissioner of New York city.

James K. Paulding, author and secretary of the Allied Hospitals of New York.

J. Van Viechen Olcott, congressman.

Phelps Phelps, assemblyman.

Howard C. Forbes, food administrator.

MERCHANTS

F. N. Abercrombie of Abercrombie & Fish, New York.

Thomas H. Silver, Lumber Insurance Company.

Conrad N. Pitcher, head of Pitcher Lumber Corporation. Stacy W. Arrowood, wool merchant, Worth street, New York city.

H. Murray Lamont, broker.

Louis Guenther, editor and publisher of *Financial World*.

Stanley H. Howe, head of Welfare commission under Mayor Mitchel.

George Hiram Mann, constitutional lawyer and head of Widows' Pensions Association.

J. H. Eisinger, head worker, University Settlement Society.

Mrs. Ray F. Schwartz, head worker, Y.W.H.A.

Marcus M. Marks, former president, borough of Manhattan.

E. H. Boyezen, firm of Sullivan & Cromwell.

Harold A. Content, former assistant U.S. Attorney.

George W. Morgan, former superintendent of elections and partner of William C. Breed, president of New York Bar Association.

John F. Curry, commissioner of records, New York city.

James P. Sinnott, secretary police department, New York city.

President Jacob Ruppert, New York Yankees.

President Charles A. Stoneham, New York Giants.

Vice President Branch Rickey, St. Louis Cardinals.

President Thomas Shibe, Philadelphia Athletics.

Connie Mack, manager, Philadelphia Athletics.

President C. H. McDiarmid, Cincinnati National League Baseball Club.
President Frank J. Nevin, Detroit National League Baseball Club.
President Barney Dreyfus, Pittsburgh American League Baseball Club.

ADAMS'S STATEMENT

The Adams statement follows:

"Boston, by reputation, is a city of true sportsmanship and high ideals and as such will not permit to go unrebuked any injustice or unfair play.

"During my brief absence from the city I find that unfounded as well as untruthful charges directed at my associate, Judge Emil E. Fuchs, president of the Boston National League Baseball club, were permitted in evidence at a public hearing and in consequence broadcast by publication throughout the length and breadth of the land.

"To me, Judge Fuchs has proven himself a gentleman, charitable to a fault, and so modest by nature that he has not fully replied to these charges.

"A sense of personal responsibility has prompted me to act in this matter, knowing full well he will not attempt to establish in his own behalf a lifelong record of honorable and admirable conduct.

"Immediately on my arrival in New York I was acquainted with the developments during my absence, and the spirit of justice could not permit me to remain idle. In a few hours the endorsements furnished herewith were obtained, and I know from that brief experience, were it necessary, that hundreds of similar testimonials can be added.

FROM ALL SIDES

"From civic leaders, from bench and bar, from banker and settlement worker, irrespective of race or creed poured forth unreservedly tributes of confidence gained from long acquaintance and association. From youth to manhood it was the same story of Emil Fuchs, flawless, lovable, kind and charitable — in magnificent tribute.

"We, of Boston, should gladly support and defend such men whether in sport or in business or in civic life, in our efforts to make this world a better and happier place in which to live.

"The results of the hurried effort in behalf of my friend are ample answer to any of the charges made involving him, including the statement that he intended to mulct me of $100,000 for his own enrichment. Such a statement, as well as the other charges, were vicious falsehoods. Judge Fuch's ideals never have changed during our acquaintance, and from the start of the Sunday baseball campaign he consistently maintained this principle, 'not a dishonest penny to be given or spent directly or indirectly.'"

SMITH'S TELEGRAM

The telegram by Ex-Gov. Alfred E. Smith, which is typical of the scores submitted to the finance commission, read as follows:

"I have known Emil E. Fuchs for more than 25 years, during all of which time he was a respectable citizen of New York and much esteemed by bench and bar as well as by leading citizens of both political parties."

The telegram of Mayor Walker of New York read:

"In official and private life in New York, Judge Emil E. Fuchs, after many years of acquaintance, I can attest to his splendid integrity, high standard of conduct and fine reputation for veracity."

Horace White, governor of state of New York succeeding Gov. Hughes:

"I have known Judge Emil Fuchs well, professionally and personally, and have been acquainted with his character and reputation many years. Have great respect for him and know that he bears high reputation as jurist and citizen."

Jacob B. Banton, district attorney of New York county for the past eight years, and previously assistant attorney:

"I have known Judge Fuchs for a generation. During his career in New York, professionally, judicially, as deputy attorney-general, and in private life, am glad to attest to his high character and integrity, and to my confidence and faith in her veracity and fairness."

FROM EX–POLICE HEAD

This telegram was also signed by the following judges of the court of general sessions, the highest criminal tribunal in New York city: Judges Charles C. Nott, Jr., Cornelius F. Follins, Joseph Mulqueen, Morris Koenig and Otto Rosalsky. It was further attended to by Isidore Waservogal, justice of the supreme court and former Secretary of State Samuel S. Koenig.

Former Police Commissioner Richard E. Enright of New York:

"Judge Emil E. Fuchs known to me since boyhood and well known in New York. His record and character as a citizen, a lawyer and a judge is above reproach. No man stands higher in this community than Judge Fuchs."

"Roxy," widely known theatrical man: "I have known Judge Emil E. Fuchs intimately for the past 10 years and know his family. He is an honored and welcome guest in my home and is incapable of doing a mean or selfish act. His many friends here in New York greatly resent any implication against his character. We know him to be a regular fellow, with a heart as big as a mountain, whose integrity has never been questioned."

Robert Adamson, ex–fire commissioner of New York, now vice president of the Bank of the United States:

"I have known Judge Emil E. Fuchs, both in private and public life for the past 25 years, and unhesitatingly say that I regard him as a man of strict honor and integrity."

Judge George Vincent Mullin of the New York superior court:

"I have known Emil Fuchs intimately for 16 years. I have appointed him referee and receiver. I have the highest opinion of his character and would trust him implicitly, to do the right thing in any situation. I stand ready to furnish further and more detailed testimonials if desired."

Leroy Scott, president of the Authors' Society of America:

"I have known Emil Fuchs most intimately for over 25 years in all kinds of circumstances. I have always found him honest, of high integrity, with a fine distinction between right and wrong, which is a policy he has carried into every-day practice. I shall always honor Emil Fuchs as one man who helps professional sports by bringing real prestige and dignity into this American pastime."

John A. Heydler, president of the National league:

"I am glad to state that in my official dealings with Judge Fuchs during the past six years, I have found him to be trustworthy and honorable and always ready to support any movement for the best interest of the game."

James McDonough, vice president of the Manufacturers Trust Company, New York:

"Have known Emil Fuchs in business and socially for many years. Have found him to be honorable, truthful, trustworthy, and of splendid character both in public and private."

William M. Calder, United States senator from New York, 1912–1923:

"I have known Emil Fuchs for the past 20 years. He is a man of the highest integrity, whose private and public life has never been questioned. I am pleased to number him among my friends."

Mrs. Ray F. Schwartz, head worker of the Y.W.H.A., New York:

"As a warm and very close personal friend of Judge Emil E. Fuchs for more than 30 years, I am glad to testify that he has been a true friend to all who know him, a faithful and devoted husband and father, and a truly loyal citizen."

Charles E. Heydt, vice president of the Bank of the United States:

"I have known Judge Emil Fuchs for twenty years, in intimate contact with him professionally and socially, and have never known him to do any act which might be subject to criticism. I always have had the highest regard and opinion of his character, integrity and veracity. He has served here in public office with honor and distinction."

FROM ST. LOUIS CLUB

Branch Rickey, vice president of the St. Louis National baseball club:

"I want you to have the assurance of myself and the St. Louis club of the high regard in which we hold Judge Fuchs. We believe him to be a true sportsman, honest and straightforward in his dealings. Our confidence in his integrity is in no way disturbed by the present controversy."

A telegram, dated Jan. 21, 1929, read:

"We have all known Emil Fuchs for many years and most cordially testify to his character, sterling worth, and integrity. F. N. Abercrombie, Abercrombie & Finch, New York city; J. Van Viechen Olcott, congressman; Howard C. Forbes, head administrator of foods, state of New York; Phelps Phelps, assemblyman.

"H. Murray Lamont, broker, New York City; Conrad N. Pitcher, head of lumber corporation; Stanley H. Howe, head of welfare commission under Mayor John E. Mitchel; Thomas H. Silver, vice president, Lumber Insurance Company; Stacy Arrowood, wool merchant, New York city; Louis Guenther, editor and publisher, *Financial World.*"

BY FORMER AMBASSADOR

James R. Sheffield, ambassador to Mexico, 1924–1928:

"There has been brought to my attention through the press, statements involving Judge Fuchs with relation to the Outdoor Recreation League, and some reflections upon his character and reputation during the many years I have known him in New York.

"Of the Outdoor Recreation League matters I know little, but it is inconceivable to me that a man of his character, his knowledge of the law, and his desire to further wholesome outdoor sport could have knowingly violated any statute of Massachusetts. I am chiefly interested, however, in the other charges that have been made, or rather, perhaps, insinuations against him, because with reference to these things I can speak with knowledge and assurance.

"I have known Judge Fuchs for over 25 years. In public office and out of it, in connection with the interests of the Republican party in which he took an active part, in connection with his work as deputy attorney-general of the state of New York and as a city magistrate and in many other ways, I have never known him to be actuated in public or private life by anything except the highest of motives. In character and loyalty to every interest placed in his charge whether legal or personal, he has proved himself of the highest type of man and citizen."

FROM McADOO

Prof. Frank E. Sommer, dean of New York University school of law:

"Emil Fuchs, a graduate of this school, possesses all of the qualities required to fulfill any high judicial office, by character, ability and training."

Chief Justice William G. McAdoo:

"I cannot allow Judge Fuchs to resign from this court without expressing my respect for the judicial and personal qualities of a high order which he has brought to the performance of his duty as a magistrate. He has displayed in an unusual degree learning in the law, patience, forbearance and courage and a proper conception of the responsibilities, honors and, in a better sense, benevolent opportunities of this very important office. During his term I have come to regard him as a man of unusual attainments intellectually and amiable qualities of loyal friendships."

Col. William Hayward, department of justice, United States attorney's office:

"I believe you thoroughly qualified in every respect for the office of justice of the general sessions, and will be happy to support you personally."

FROM CONNIE MACK

Connie Mack, treasurer and manager of the Philadelphia American League Baseball Club:

"I have been in close touch with Judge Emil Fuchs ever since he became connected with baseball and found him to be a man whose words can be absolutely relied upon. He is one of those fine characters who does so much to make life enjoyable for others. In my contact with Judge Fuchs I have found him 100 per cent."

Charles A. Stoneham, president of New York Giants:

"Long before I became personally acquainted with Judge Emil E. Fuchs I had known of his reputation as a man of high integrity and character. I never fully appreciated what this meant until I had the pleasure of knowing him personally, and since during that time I can certify that such reputation was fully justified."

Jacob Ruppert, president of New York Yankees:

"I have known Judge Emil Fuchs for a number of years and it is with pleasure that I certify to his high character, his reputation for truth and veracity and for honest dealings. His both public and private life is unquestioned. I hold him in the highest esteem, and consider him to be a gentleman in the best sense of the word."

FROM SCHWAB

Charles M. Schwab, director-general of the United States shipping board during the war, and present chairman of the board of Bethlehem Steel Company:

"I am taking the liberty of sending you this message in behalf of my good friend, Hon. Emil Fuchs, whom it has been my pleasure to know for many years. I have always esteemed his friendship, knowing him to be a man of integrity and of the highest motives."

C. J. McDiarmit, president of Cincinnati National League Baseball Club:

"Association with Judge Fuchs for several years last past have given me a very high regard for his integrity, his conduct, and eminent sense of fairness. Any statement to the contrary would not be believed by me. Generosity and fairness are inborn in him. Possibly too generous for his own material welfare, but fair and square beyond any question."

Frank J. Nevin, president Detroit American League Baseball Club:

"In justice to Judge Fuchs, I have known him for a number of years and have never heard anything except that his character and reputation for fair dealing is of the highest. Members of both leagues are always impressed with his attitude, vision and character in baseball."

BY BARNEY DREYFUS

Barney Dreyfus, president of Pittsburgh National League Baseball Club:

"Sincerely regret attack upon the character of Judge Fuchs. As long as I have known him I have found him to be absolutely honorable and upright in all his dealings, and I believe his integrity to be above reproach. If truth and justice prevail, I know he will be vindicated."

United States Senator Robert F. Wagner of New York:

"I have known Judge Fuchs a number of years. He and I are members of opposite political parties, but he has always been held in high esteem in New York and bears a very good reputation."

Fr. Francis P. Duffey, chaplain of the 27th division during the war:

"I know Judge Fuchs well. I have a high regard for him and he bears an excellent reputation as to honesty and veracity in private and public life."

Thomas S. Shibe, president, Philadelphia American League Baseball Club:

"I have been in personal contact with Judge Emil Fuchs since he has been connected with baseball and have found him to be a man of his word and honest in all his dealings."

Mgr. Curry, Holy Name Church, New York city:

"Kindly add my testimony of the splendid personal worth of Mr. Fuchs, always square, above board, and always ready to help others. Our friendship is existing for about 18 years."

MAN OF HIS WORD

Emory R. Buckner, United States district attorney of New York, succeeding Col. Hayward, until the beginning of 1938 and appointed by Gov. Smith, who prosecuted the Queens county scandal:

"I have known Emil Fuchs for 20 years. My acquaintance with him has been a personal one and not casually limited to professional contacts. He has always shown himself to be a man of his word and integrity, which opinion is shared by the community."

Col. Robert Guggenheim of the Guggenheim Foundation:

"I have never known anyone of higher character or better reputation and more veracious than Judge Emil Fuchs. I have just heard of the shameful attack on his character, and in all the years that I have known him he has never done a single unkind act or anything to warrant even reproach."

Charles D. Hilles, secretary to the President of the United States in the administration of William Howard Taft and national committeeman from the state of New York:

"In response to your request for my estimate of Emil Fuchs, I take pleasure in saying that I have known him for 15 years and regard him highly.

"He was a deputy attorney-general of the state from 1900 to 1910, serving under three administrations. He was in the active practice here from 1910 until 1916, when he became a city magistrate. He continued in that court for two years, resigning voluntarily. His associates in that court, particularly Chief Judge McAdoo, held him in high esteem.

"He was a devoted friend of the late Job E. Hedges. I know that Mr. Hedges entertained both admiration and affectionate regard for him. He was also a close friend of the late Republican state chairman, George Glynn.

"Both these men told me repeatedly that they knew that Judge Fuchs was actuated by high motives.

"From my acquaintance with him and his family, and my knowledge of his devotion to his family, it would be difficult for me to believe that he would knowingly engage in any transaction that would reflect discredit upon his family."

Appendix B

Wally Berger is one of the most underestimated, unsung heroes in baseball and one of its nicest in both his personal and professional life.

His slugging percentage for 10 years in the majors was .522. Only 27 players in the history of baseball have posted a higher number. During the same period he maintained a batting average of .300. Fewer than 3 percent of all baseball players became members of the "Three Hundred Club." He was a superb fielder; due to his extraordinary speed he made what would have been spectacular catches look routine. He ranks among the top 20 players in career putouts and total chances per game.

"Letters between the Judge and Wally Berger presented here are reprinted with permission from *Freshly Remembered* written and published in collaboration with Berger by his friend, George Snyder":

BOSTON NATIONAL LEAGUE BASEBALL COMPANY
BRAVES FIELD, BOSTON

January 13, 1930

Mr. Walter Berger
406 East 42nd St.
Los Angeles, Calif.

Dear Mr. Berger:
Enclosed please find contract for $750 per month, which represents the usual increase over the salary received from your former club, with a hope that your work will warrant a far more substantial increase in your contract for 1931.

Please sign contract and return at your earliest convenience, reporting to Manager McKechnie, at the West Coast Inn (opposite the ball park), St. Petersburg, Fla., on February 28th. Your transportation will be returned to you by Mr. Cunningham, our secretary, on your arrival.

Wishing you a happy and successful new year, I am,

Sincerely yours,

(s) Emil E. Fuchs
President

BOSTON NATIONAL LEAGUE BASEBALL COMPANY
BRAVES FIELD, BOSTON

January 8, 1931

Mr. Walter Berger
445 1/2 E. 43rd St.
Los Angeles, Calif.

Dear Walter:

Enclosed please find a contract for $7000, which is an increase of $3000 over last year's contract.

I went over the situation with Manager McKechnie and we both appreciate that you, for a first year man, made a very creditable showing. I am personally adding an extra $500, which I do not desire to have appear in the contract, but upon the signing of same by you we shall mail you a check for $500, which is my method of giving you an extra reward for your diligent, faithful service and as a medium of encouragement to you.

My methods with reference to salaries has always been to give the players who remain with us some increase each year, depending, of course, upon their ability, deportment, and value to the club. You can readily understand, therefore, that with an increase as substantial as the enclosed, if you can show the progress already indicated by you, you can anticipate a further increase each year as time goes on, which I hope will put you in a position of being one of the well paid ball players in the major leagues.

There is nothing further to add except that I believe you will appreciate our desire to be entirely fair with you, and therefore you will also understand that the enclosed contract, which we hope will be satisfactory to you, is a final one. My method has been and always will be to give what I think is fair, to avoid any future correspondence and disputes.

Judge Landis phoned about your playing ball during this last month on the coast, which, of course, is contrary to baseball law. I wired him that in my opinion you had misinterpreted and misunderstood the rule.

I hope that you will continue to have a pleasant winter and that we shall meet at St. Petersburg, where you will please report to Manager McKechnie at the West Coast Inn on the morning of Wednesday, February 25th.

With warm regards to Mrs. Berger, I am,

Sincerely yours,

(s) Emil E. Fuchs
President

P.S. Please return signed contract immediately in order that Manager McKechnie may determine on whom he can count, as this year's rule prohibits any player from spring training camp whose contract is unsigned. You will be reimbursed by Secretary Cunningham upon your arrival for any money advanced by you for transportation expense.

3125 Hollydale Dr.
Los Angeles, Calif.
Jan. 15, 1931

Dear Judge:

Contract and letter received and appreciate your attitude toward the increase of your players' salary. It's only reasonable that a player expects an increase each year, but each case is different and I believe that if you'll look into my case further you can readily see my reasons for feeling that the increase offered me is not sufficient.

Now, if we were taking last year's salary as a basis it would be a very nice increase but I really don't feel that we should do that.

Last year if you'll remember I received practically no increase over my Coast League contract and accepted rather than argue so I could prove that I was of Major League ability.

I never have felt that I received my true worth last season so you can see why I don't feel that any increase with last season's salary as a basis is fair to me.

In regards to the 500 dollar bonus offered to me I had felt that I was deserving of a bonus for last season's work, so feel that your offer of that is for work done in the past and I assure you that the offer certainly is appreciated and lives up to your reputation for fairness.

I think that the amount tendered me for the coming year should be as to my true worth to the club and not an increase over last year's contract.

I know the amount that I am asking of you sounds like a large jump but I feel that I drew enough fans through the gate and was popular enough with the Boston fans to be worth $10,000 a year to your club. Now Judge don't think me fat-headed but just look things over and if you were in my position. Would you take a cent less than $10,000 a year?

Hoping to hear favorably from you and best regards to everyone in the office. I am,

Sincerely yours,

Walter Berger

BOSTON NATIONAL LEAGUE BASEBALL COMPANY
BRAVES FIELD, BOSTON

January 28, 1931

Mr. Walter Berger
3125 Hollydale Dr.,
Los Angeles, Calif.

Dear Walter:

Thank you for your nice letter of January 15th. Your argument is a very reasonable one in theory. In other words, if you had received a larger amount in accordance with your work, last year's contract would have been higher, and by the same process of fair increase, so would this year's contract have been larger, but let me tell you for your information, so that you are not misled, that no second year man in the history of baseball, that I know of or am able to learn of, ever received a $10,000 contract for his second year's services.

I believe that Manager McKechnie, who is intensely interested in your career and your future with him and the club, will tell you that. I have again talked with him and he is endeavoring to give you the benefit of every opportunity and advance possible. He feels that you have been fairly and justly treated, and so do I. My policy has always been to increase the salaries of my players as long as they are loyal, keep their heads, and so conduct themselves as to permit an increase.

You have a long way to go in baseball, and it is our hope that your last year's work will be improved upon in 1931, all of which will be appreciated and demonstrated by another increase, and more as the years go by. I honestly believe that if you were acquainted with the conditions that bring about large salaries, you would find that they come gradually and are based on justice to the player.

You mention in your letter what I would do if I were in your position. Inasmuch as you make that statement I will answer it — if I were in your position, having in mind your youth and physical ability, I would sign the contract, say nothing more about it, remain the same modest young man that you have been, and demonstrate your right to the same consideration next year that you have received this. That is all that I can say or advise you on.

We must adopt a policy which we think is fair and stand by it; therefore I hope that you will follow the advice that you seek so that the relationship between you and the club can go on for years to come in the same pleasant manner.

Sincerely yours,

(s) Emil E. Fuchs
President

———————

3125 Hollydale Dr.
Los Angeles, Calif.
Feb. 3, 1931

Mr. Emil E. Fuchs,
Braves Field
Boston, Mass.

Dear Judge:

Your letter of the 28th received and am glad to know that you can at least see a part of my reasons for not signing the contract you have offered me.

I don't care to go into what other players have or do receive, their affairs have nothing to do with what I do. I can only bank my own check and that is what I'm interested in. As far as no other player receiving $10,000 a year in his second year, you know Judge, that there is always a first time for everything, and if I didn't feel that I was worth that amount, I wouldn't be asking for it.

I appreciate the interest that both you and Bill McKechnie have taken in my playing and also the advice you have given me regarding the contract, but Judge, I don't believe you put yourself in my position when you wrote that.

If I signed that contract as you suggest, I would not be satisfied and I don't think that you would want anyone on your club that was not entirely satisfied with his contract.

I want you still to feel that I am the same modest fellow that I have always been but that I do feel that I am worth $10,000 a year to your club with that modesty. I sincerely hope that you will think over my case some more and can see your way to give me the increase that I think I should get.

This part of the game is strictly business proposition and while it may sound egotistical I think you will take it only as I mean it.

I think the Boston Club made money last year and I believe that I helped make it and am entitled to the increase.

Sincerely yours,

Walter Berger

WESTERN UNION

BOSTON MASS

1931 FEB 12 AM 11 24

WALTER BERGER
3125 HOLLYDALE DR
LOS ANGELES CALIF

INASMUCH AS I WANT YOU THOROUGHLY SATISFIED I AM BREAKING A RULE IN GIVING YOU CONTRACT FOR SEVENTY FIVE HUNDRED AND ONE THOUSAND FOR SIGNING WILL BE COMPELLED TO DO WITHOUT YOUR SERVICES UNLESS YOU ACCEPT THESE TERMS

EMIL E FUCHS

BOSTON NATIONAL LEAGUE BASEBALL COMPANY
BRAVES FIELD, BOSTON

Jan. 22, 1932

Mr. Walter Berger,
3125 Hollydale Drive,
Los Angeles, Calif.

Dear Walter:

Enclosed please find contract for 1932 calling for $10,000 for the season. In view of all conditions I am sure you will agree with us is reasonable in accordance with my promise in last year's correspondence.

With warm regards to you and Mrs. Berger, I am

Sincerely yours,

(s) Emil E. Fuchs
President

Please report at the West Coast Inn, St. Petersburg Florida on March 1st. Pay transportation, including Pullman, and this will be refunded on arrival by Secretary Cunningham. Meal allowance while traveling will be at the rate of $4.00 per day.

St. Petersburg, Fla.
Feb. 19, 1932

Mr. Emil E. Fuchs,
Braves Field,
Boston, Mass.

Dear Judge:
Received contract and letter and appreciate your attitude toward the increase in salary.

It is only within reason for a player to expect an increase with each successful year and the size of the increase in accordance to the value that he is to the club. In my case the amount tendered to me is not quite sufficient.

I [came] through with another successful year, a better one in fact than the preceding one. I feel that I drew enough people at the gate and was popular enough with the Boston fans to be worth $12,000 a year to your club.

Now Judge, don't think I'm getting egotistical take this as a business proposition.

Hoping to hear favorably from you and with best regards to the gang at the office, I am

Sincerely yours,

Walter Berger

BOSTON NATIONAL LEAGUE BASEBALL COMPANY
BRAVES FIELD, BOSTON

St. Petersburg, Fla.
March 23rd 1932

Mr. Walter Berger,
St. Petersburg, Fla.

Dear Walter:
You are holding up a large number of contracts, which are all signed and completed, yours being the only one outstanding.

I hope and expect that our relationship will continue to be amicable and pleasant and my personal opinion is that you will do far better being guided by one, who always has had his players' welfare in mind.

The player who holds out annually sometimes gets the shade the better of it but my experience is that in the end such demands are not forgotten and he generally loses by total.

Not only as a matter of comparison but for the reason as I explained to you that we expect you to be with the Braves a great many years, your salary both as a matter of duration and ability, will compare favorably with any one in the league, irrespective of club he may be on.

As we decided that the salary offered you for the coming season, every thing taken into consideration, is just and fair, it will not serve your best purpose to delay signing any longer.

Therefore, I must request that you sign same immediately and give same to Mr. Cunningham.

Very truly yours,

(s) Emil E. Fuchs
President

BOSTON NATIONAL LEAGUE BASEBALL COMPANY
BRAVES FIELD, BOSTON

January 11, 1933

Mr. Walter Berger,
5915 So. Wilton Pl.
Los Angeles, Calif.

My dear Walter:
We are endeavoring to demonstrate the falsity of the general impression that ball players are unconcerned as to what happens to the fortunes or misfortunes that befall an investor and stockholder of a ball club today.

We contend that the intelligent players know what is happening, not only in this country but throughout the civilized world, and therefore our Board of Directors, instead of placing an arbitrary figure of reduction, would like to point out to the baseball world that the members of the Braves team cooperated in a voluntary and reasonable cut to meet the depression conditions existing.

The example that was set in Baseball must appeal to every thoughtful unit, either making a livelihood from or interested in the national game. Judge Landis starts by voluntarily refusing to draw more than a nominal sum, so that the necessary functioning of his office may properly continue. President John A. Heydler voluntarily has reduced his own salary eighteen percent.

The president of your club has voluntarily reduced his salary twenty percent. Your manager, who has a written contract, has volunteered to reduce his salary upwards of ten percent.

The new players who are joining the Braves have already signified their desire to be recorded in favor of a reduction over their previous contracts elsewhere.

Every business enterprise in the country has either arbitrarily, or by general consent, reduced salaries from twenty to thirty percent. The minor leagues have reduced their salary limit over fifty percent. The various leagues, major and minor, have reduced their appropriation from twenty to forty percent. Every club of the major leagues has pledged itself to a largely reduced pay roll. In one of the outstanding clubs of this country, the players have voluntarily agreed to a substantial reduction, so that the Boston club, when all is said and done, will be found to have reduced less, and will not alter their custom of increasing the very low paid men so as to encourage them with a livable wage in spite of the depression.

I want you to have the following facts in mind when you answer this letter:

First — that we appreciate your efforts.

Second — that we have no complaint as to your playing ability and your showing.

Third — in 1931 and 1932 we had over half a million people attending our home games, but the stockholders have not yet been able to draw a dividend or a single dollar interest on their investment since their connection.

Fourth — If times and conditions are such in 1933 that the stockholders are able to draw 4 percent on the capital stock, whatever reduction you make in your contract this year will be given to you at the end of the 1933 season, and if times are better, the normal increase based on your work, will continue.

Fifth — In order for the stockholders to accomplish this modest end, the attendance at Braves Field for the year 1933 must total 650,000. This in ordinary times, should not be a hard task, if with our increased strength we can remain in the first division. In that event you are to keep this letter as evidence of our promise to refund to you any reduction from your 1932 contract.

I am confident your action will be such as to enable our club to point with pride to your cooperation and understanding.

Please answer this at once.

Very truly yours,

(s) Emil E. Fuchs
President

BOSTON NATIONAL LEAGUE BASEBALL COMPANY
BRAVES FIELD, BOSTON

January 31, 1933

Mr. Walter Berger,
5915 So. Wilton Pl.
Los Angeles, Calif.

Dear Walter:

I wrote you a letter, which I take it you have not yet received, owing perhaps to your not having been at home, but I believe if you had received it, you would have voluntarily suggested a contract such as the enclosed, i.e., $9000 for the season of 1933.

As February is here, I cannot wait longer for your voluntary suggestion, and, therefore, tender you a contract which was decided at a meeting of the Board of Directors as being fair, equitable and final.

I wish you would read my letter so that you can again appreciate what is going on. A $9000 contract in these times, where you are sure of receiving that amount in cash, is equal to $15,000 in normal times, and I therefore will ask you to kindly sign and return it at your earliest convenience, reporting to Manager McKechnie at the West Coast Inn, St. Petersburg, on the morning of March 6th.

With all good wishes, I am,

Very truly yours,

(s) Emil E. Fuchs
President

P.S. Kindly pay your own transportation; it will be refunded to you by Secretary Cunningham on your arrival at St. Petersburg.

Culver City, California
Feb. 3, 1931

Mr. Emil E. Fuchs, President
Boston Braves,
Braves Field,
Boston, Massachusetts

Dear Judge:
Contract received. After due consideration I find the terms unsatisfactory and do not intend to take a cut in salary for the coming season.

I had a good season last year and expected a raise. In our talks last spring about contracts you impressed on me that I was going to be with your club for years, and after each successful year I was to get an increase in salary. You also told me that your policy was not to give large increases, but a fair one, and in time I would be better off, etc. I suppose you have forgotten all about that. I have not!

Inasmuch that I expected an increase, Judge, I will sign for the same salary as last year, and consider that I have received a cut in salary. This depression has not cut my expenses very much, and I will not go into lengthy detail to explain why at this time.

Don't believe that I am being unreasonable in asking for the same money that I received last year, and please consider this as my final proposition.

Hoping to have a favorable reply, I am,

Very truly yours,

Walter Berger

P.S. My present address is 4049 Madison Avenue, c/o Morse Apartment, Apt. #203., Culver City, Calif.

POSTAL TELEGRAPH

FEB 24 1933

WALTER A BERGER=
APT 203 4049 MADISON AVE CULVERCITY CALIF=

WE WIRED YOU TO REPORT ON TIME AND WE WOULD TREAT YOU FAIRLY AND THEREFORE EXPECT YOU TO REPORT ACCORDING=

EMILE E FUCHS

BOSTON NATIONAL LEAGUE BASEBALL COMPANY
BRAVES FIELD, BOSTON

August 25, 1933

Mr. Walter Berger,
c/o Boston Braves,
Boston.

My dear Walter:

Owing to the bad start we had this year, we would have to draw between now and the 3rd of September upward of 160,000 people to come near the attendance of the previous years, in accordance with the promise made by Mr. Adams the gentlemen of the club who received a cut in their 1933 salary.

I believe your spirit and the spirit of the club has done so much for Boston and the Braves that irrespective of whether or not that total is reached, I feel it is justly due you for me to reinstate the amount of your 1932 contract, and you will receive the proportionate share of the amount of your cut of your salary check on the various pay days left this year. The first check to have the added share will be your salary check of September 1st.

Thanking you for your devotion both to me personally and to Mr. McKechnie, as well as to the club, and know that this action will further install in you the desire to keep up the fight, I am, with warmest regards,

Sincerely yours

(s) Emil E. Fuchs
President

BOSTON NATIONAL LEAGUE BASEBALL COMPANY
BRAVES FIELD, BOSTON

January 17, 1934

Mr. Walter Berger,
253 N. E. 14th St.,
Miami, Fla.

Dear Walter:

I enclose contract for $11,500.

I am endeavoring to be fair with each individual player and recognize your improvement last year. As soon as business conditions change, I hope to continue to improve the status of the men who are giving us the benefit of their ability, loyalty, skill and hustle.

Please sign and return the contract, for I hope you feel that my action entitles me to no further controversy, and if anything, your approval.

Sincerely yours,

(s) Emil E. Fuchs
President

Suite 229, Hotel Touraine,
Boston

Copley Plaza Hotel
Suite 19

January 28, 1935

Mr. Walter Berger,
3928 Sixth Ave.,
Los Angeles, Calif.

Dear Walter:

In spite of the large losses of the club last year, the bill which you mailed will be paid, as we are re-financing the club, and there will be no future danger of holding up even small bills.

Enclosed you will find a contract for $12,000 and there will absolutely be no use in arguing about it. The club is endeavoring to pay as much as any other club, but in the event that it may be, in your opinion, less than what you would obtain elsewhere, remember this — in the expenditure of hundreds of thousands of dollars, we are entitled to have a few ball players who can make good without insisting that they obtain contracts which cannot be met with the limited attendance.

If 1935 turns out right, and your record is good, you will have a good argument in 1936, but I will ask you to immediately sign this contract and return it, so that I may be able to say to the public that our players have met the spirit of our efforts to continue baseball here on a high plane.

With warm regards to Mrs. Berger and yourself, I am,

Sincerely yours,

(s) Emil E. Fuchs
President

P.S. Kindly report for training at the West Coast Inn, St. Petersburg, on Thursday, February 28th.

February 7, 1935

Mr. Walter Berger,
3928 Sixth Ave.,
Los Angeles, Calif.

Dear Walter:
   I received your very kind letter, together with your contract, and I assure you, as time goes on, you will not regret your consideration and the kind message received today.

   With warmest regards and best wishes to you both, I am,

Sincerely yours,

(s) Emil E. Fuchs
President

February 11, 1935

Mr. Walter Berger,
3928 Sixth Ave.,
Los Angeles, Calif.

My dear Walter:
   I do not have the exact amount of the outlay agreed upon between us, but I know it was something around this figure, and if you have not already received it, I shall ask you to let me know the exact amount. If it is overpaid you can return it to the club; if underpaid, we will pay you the balance.

Sincerely yours,

(s) Emil E. Fuchs
President

Appendix C

Winners of the Judge Emil Fuchs Memorial Award

1959 Ernie Banks*	1979 Willie Mays*
1960 Larry Sherry	1980 Earl Weaver
1961 Dick Groat	1981 Bill Veeck
1962 Bill McKechnie*	1982 Frank Robinson*
1963 Jack Sanford	1983 Brooks Robinson*
1964 Bill Monbouquette	1984 Luis Aparicio*
1965 John Quinn	1985 Ralph Houk
1966 Walter Alston*	1986 Calvin Griffith
1967 Gabe Paul	1987 Birdie Tebbetts
1968 Bob Gibson*	1988 Tom Seaver*
1969 Carl Yastrzemski*	1989 Johnny Pesky
1970 Joe Cronin*	1990 Bill White
1971 Dick O'Connell	1991 Joe Morgan
1972 Duffy Lewis	1992 Dick Williams
1973 Warren Spahn*	1993 Don Zimmer
1974 Hank Aaron*	1994 Haywood Sullivan
1975 Whitey Ford*	1995 Sam Mele
1976 Robin Roberts*	1996 Tommy Holmes
1977 Eddie Mathews*	1997 Lou Gorman
1978 Rod Carew*	

Members of the Baseball Hall of Fame

Index